Edward Bell, Charlotte Anne Waldie Eaton

Waterloo days

The narrative of an Englishwoman resident at Brussels in June 1815

Edward Bell, Charlotte Anne Waldie Eaton

Waterloo days
The narrative of an Englishwoman resident at Brussels in June 1815

ISBN/EAN: 9783337141660

Printed in Europe, USA, Canada, Australia, Japan

Cover: Foto ©Andreas Hilbeck / pixelio.de

More available books at **www.hansebooks.com**

WATERLOO DAYS;

THE NARRATIVE OF AN ENGLISHWOMAN
RESIDENT AT BRUSSELS IN JUNE, 1815.

BY

CHARLOTTE A. EATON,

AUTHOR OF "ROME IN THE NINETEENTH CENTURY,"
"AT HOME AND ABROAD,"
ETC.

NEW EDITION.

WITH AN INTRODUCTION AND APPENDIX
BY EDWARD BELL, M.A.

LONDON: GEORGE BELL & SONS, YORK STREET,
COVENT GARDEN.
1888.

INTRODUCTION.*

THE following little book which was first published within two years of the events which it describes, was republished in 1852, after some revision by the author, under the title of "The Days of Battle." It has now been out of print for a considerable time, but its merits as a very graphic and interesting description of those few momentous days which have left their mark on English· literature no less than on the history of Europe, are sufficient, it is believed, to justify its republication in a popular series.

Though it was first published anonymously as a " Narrative of a few days' Residence in Belgium with some account of a visit to the field of Waterloo, by an Englishwoman," it has so much personal interest that the reader will, doubtless, be glad to know something of its author, more especially as she is favourably known by other works, and with other members of her family has claims upon the memory of a younger generation.

Miss Charlotte Anne Waldie, the lady in question, was born 28 September, 1788, and was the second of three daughters

---

* I have to thank Mr. C. O. Eaton, J.P., of Tolethorpe Hall, Stamford, for his assistance in preparing this account of his mother's various writings ; and Mr. George Hooper, author of " Waterloo, the Downfall of the First Napoleon," for kindly revising the notes at the end of the volume.

of George Waldie, Esq., of Hendersyde Park, near Kelso, Roxburghshire, and Forth House, Newcastle-on-Tyne. There were also two sons, one of whom is mentioned in the following pages, but they both died without issue. The eldest daughter, Maria Jane, married in 1812 Mr. Richard Griffith, the distinguished civil engineer, who was appointed by Government sole commissioner for the general valuation of Ireland, and was the author of the famous geological map of that country. After more than forty years of arduous public service, during a large part of which he was President of the Board of Works in Ireland, he was created a baronet; and his son, Sir George R. Waldie-Griffith, inherited Mr. Waldie's estates.

The youngest of the three sisters, Jane, was an accomplished painter, and her pictures are to be met with in many institutions in the north of England. She also had considerable literary talent, and wrote a work entitled "Sketches descriptive of Italy," which was published in four volumes in 1820. She married Captain, afterwards Admiral, Watts, of Langton Grange, near Staindrop, Darlington, but unfortunately died in early life.

Charlotte, the sister with whom we are chiefly concerned, accompanied her brother and younger sister, as is hereafter related, on a visit to Brussels, in June, 1815, when it had temporarily and hastily become the headquarters of the army under Wellington. The allied forces, as every one supposed, were to meet and crush Napoleon, who had just returned from Elba, before he had time to take the offensive. But his movements were more rapid than had been anticipated, and the Belgian capital, crowded with non-combatants of both sexes, instead of being merely a point of departure, suddenly found itself the central point of the seat of war. The pen of Thackeray has well adapted this dramatic situation to the purposes of fiction; but in the following pages we have the circumstances brought before us with all the vividness which actual experience only can give. A few weeks later the two sisters visited the field of Waterloo, and a short narrative of the battle written by one, and illustrated by the pencil of the other, was published anonymously by Murray, and rapidly went through ten editions.

In the course of the next year the two sisters rejoined their brother in France, and went on with him to Italy, and it was then, as explained in the author's preface, that the following account, which incorporated the previous narrative, made its appearance.

In 1817–18 Miss Charlotte Waldie was again in Italy, and in 1820 published, still anonymously, her best known work, "Rome in the Nineteenth Century."* This work gives the result of her own experience and observation, and is written in the personal style which, when it is combined, as in her case it is, with cultivated taste and sensible criticism, is not to be equalled in interest by any formal description. Notwithstanding the many changes which recent research and excavation have wrought in the descriptive topography of Rome the book is still useful to travellers, and is largely quoted by the latest popular writer on the subject.†

In the same year her sister published her "Sketches in Italy," above referred to. Two years later Charlotte Waldie married Stephen Eaton, Esq., banker, of Stamford, and of Ketton Hall, Rutland. A few years afterwards she published a story in three volumes, entitled "Continental Adventures."

Mrs. Eaton's last work, "At Home and Abroad," was published in 1831. In 1851 she prepared a new edition, the fifth, of "Rome in the Nineteenth Century," in two volumes, with illustrations, for Bohn's Illustrated Library, and in 1852 she revised the present work for the same publisher. She died on 28 April, 1859, in the seventy-first year of her age.

The following reprint differs only from the author's last edition in respect to the title and the appended notes. It must be remembered that the few details of the battle of Waterloo are based upon the reports current at the time, and have since been supplemented or corrected in various ways. In all that came under the writer's own observation there is no room for doubt as to her correctness, and her picture of Brussels during the days of battle is corroborated by another account, also by a lady and an English writer, namely, the well-known

---

* The first edition was published by Constable, Edinburgh; a second edition was brought out by Murray in 1826.

† See "Walks in Rome," by Augustus J. C. Hare.

Fanny Burney, who was then the wife of General D'Arblay, a French officer in the service of Louis XVIII. Madame D'Arblay, being unsuccessful in an attempt to leave the city by canal-boat, spent some weeks in Brussels, but pre-occupied as she was by the absence of her husband she exercised less observation on what was going on around her, and her account is far less graphic than that of her younger fellow-countrywoman. Nor did she visit the field of battle, and realize in an equal degree the terrible penalty which war exacts from victors as well as vanquished.* Whilst military glories are held to be worthy of commemoration, it is fitting that such details should not be left untold. And in truth the campaign of Waterloo has memories which an Englishman cannot afford to lose. If a righteous and unselfish cause may hallow the horrors of those days, it is not well to ignore them altogether. If a cool and confident intrepidity on the part of a leader, if daring disregard of life in comparison with duty on the part of his officers, if resolute and patient endurance for hours, of rank and file, under repeated charge, or still more deadly storm of lead—if, in short, courage and fortitude, well employed, are virtues not yet out of date, the tale of Waterloo should still be told, and this little book, genuine as it is, has still its testimony to add thereto.

E. B.

* There is another small book published shortly before this, " A Visit to Flanders in July, 1815," by James Simpson (Edinburgh, 1815), which also gives an account of the field a few weeks after the battle. Müffling's "Passages from my Life," and Kincaird's "Adventures in the Rifle Brigade," also give some interesting details of Brussels on the eve of Waterloo.

AUTHOR'S PREFACE.

THIS little Narrative is the simple and faithful account of one who was a spectator of the scenes she describes, and a witness of the events she relates, during those days of desperate conflict and unparalleled victory which must be for ever memorable in British history, and interesting to every British heart. It was written whilst the impression of those eventful scenes was yet fresh upon the mind : and the thoughts and feelings which such awful and affecting circumstances were irresistibly calculated to inspire, were expressed without restraint, in the full security of the sympathy and approbation of the partial friends for whose perusal alone this Narrative was intended.

During the absence of the Author in Italy in 1816, the members of her family in England sent the manuscript to the late Mr. Murray, and it was already in the press before she received any intimation of its intended publication.

The Author must be permitted most earnestly to disclaim all idea of entering into competition with the writers whose talents and genius have been so well employed in describing the battle and the field of Waterloo. They were not, how-

ever, like the Author, on the spot at the time ; they were
pilgrims who afterwards visited the memorable scenes of
these glorious events, and wrote from report: they related
the past—she described the present.

Conscious of her inadequacy to a theme on which all that
can be said falls so far short of what must be felt ; impossible
as it is to do justice to the achievements of that gallant
army who have been the champions, the conquerors, and
the deliverers of the world, and to whom, under Heaven,
Europe owes her security, and England her glory—the
writer yet ventures to hope, that the generous indulgence
of a British public will be extended to this humble attempt
to record the proofs displayed on those glorious " days of
battle," of their heroic valour in combat, their noble magnanimity in victory, and their unshaken fortitude in suffering
—faintly and feebly as they are described by

AN ENGLISHWOMAN.

THE DAYS OF BATTLE.

JUNE 1815.

On Saturday, the 10th of June, 1815, my brother, my sister, and myself, sailed from the pier of Ramsgate at three in the afternoon, in company with Sir Neil Campbell, the celebrated Knight of Elba, Major Wylie, of the Royal Fusiliers, extra aide-de-camp to the Duke of Wellington, a Mr. N., an English merchant; together with an incongruous assemblage of horses, dogs, and barouches; Irish servants, French valets, and steerage passengers, too multifarious to mention, all crowded together into a wretched little packet. On Sunday evening, the 11th of June, we found ourselves, after a passage of thirty-six hours, many miles distant from Ostend, lying at anchor in a dead calm, and without a hope of reaching it till the following morning. To escape remaining another night amidst the discomforts of this packet, without food, for we had eaten up all our provisions; and without sleep, for we had experimentally proved that none was to be got, our three selves, and our three companions in misfortune, the Knight, the

B

Major, and the Merchant, embarked in a crazy little boat, about nine o'clock in a beautiful summer's evening, as the sun was sinking in golden splendour, and trusted ourselves to the mercy of the waves. The tide was running strong against the rowers, and night closed in long before we approached the shore; but though the light of the heavens had faded, the ocean was illuminated with that beautiful phosphoric fire so well known in warmer latitudes. The most brilliant magic light played upon the surface of the waters, and marked the path of our little vessel through the deep, with the softest, purest radiance; the oars seemed to be moving through liquid fire, and every drop, as it dashed from them, sparkled like the blaze of a diamond: the little rippling waves, as they curled their heads, were covered with the same transparent ethereal fire, which would mock the powers of the poet's fancy, "glancing from heaven to earth, from earth to heaven," to embody or describe. It is more like the pale beam the glow-worm sheds from his evening lamp than anything on earth, but ten thousand times more bright and more beautiful. By such a light Oberon and his Queen, attended by their band of tiny sprites, might have held their midnight revels, amidst the bowers and halls of fairyland; and by such a light, enchanted spirits in happier worlds might be supposed to slumber. This soft, transparent, *unearthly* light gleaming around us, and kindling at every touch in living brightness over the waters; the calm and glassy stillness of the wide extended ocean; the softened glow that lingered in the western sky; and the mild breath of evening, made our passage to the shore, slow as it was, most delightful. It was a night calculated to soothe every unquiet passion into rest, and in which the imagination loved to indulge in dreams of delight and beauty. The heart must have been cold that did not feel the harmony of nature, and the spirit turbulent that did not partake of its repose: everything seemed to have been touched by the hand of enchantment. But the magic spell was dissolved, and the visions of fancy faded away in a moment; for we suddenly struck upon the sands, when we seemed still far from the shore; waves of apparent fire dashed into the boat; and the sturdy sailors, abandoning their oars, seized upon us without the smallest ceremony, and carried us literally through fire and water to the beach.

Thus were we thrown, late at night, and in the dark, upon a foreign coast, uncertain which way to direct our steps through the deep, deserted, trackless sands that surrounded us; forewarned of the rapid approach of the tides upon this coast, and wholly at a loss in what direction lay the town, or how to get admittance through the sentry posts, at such an hour, if we did reach it. Yet under these appalling circumstances, I cannot say that we felt the smallest alarm, or even a momentary uncomfortable situation: we had no fear of being drowned, nor the remotest idea that any more serious mischief could befal us than spending the night upon the sands, of which, however, there seemed to be much probability. Luckily for us, this Mr. N. proved a most able pilot; he had frequently been at Ostend before, and led the way with great sagacity, in spite of the darkness in which we were involved. We were all loaded with travelling bags, or parcels of some sort, for it was with difficulty the little nut-shell of a boat contained our six selves, and all the servants were left in the vessel. We were each, therefore, obliged to carry all that we wanted of our travelling equipments;

and thus burdened, and sinking every step ankle deep in the heavy sands, we reached at last, with considerable toil, the fortifications, and were immediately hailed by the soldier on guard. We declared ourselves to be "friends," but in vain; friends or foes were all the same to the sentry; we might have lain all night in the ditch, for anything he cared; for his orders were positive, to admit no person into the garrison, without the express order of the commandant after dark. But the cocked hat, aide-de-camp's uniform, and authoritative tone of Major Wylie carried us all through. He declared " that he and his party were going to join the army with speed ;" and, although some of us must have struck the sentry as not being likely to prove a very valuable reinforcement to the troops, he did not venture to make any further opposition, and we all entered Ostend. Although we came " in such a questionable shape," we obtained admittance into " La Cour Impériale," where we got an excellent supper, which was particularly acceptable to some of us, who had eaten nothing all day, excepting a bit of bread. We then went to bed, where we enjoyed the sweets of undisturbed repose, with a zest which none but those who have spent a suffocating, sick, and sleepless night in a wretched little berth on board a packet, can understand.

Next day, after viewing the fortifications, which, although they had been recently repaired by the English, could no longer stand the long sieges which have made Ostend famous in history, we proceeded to Bruges, walked about in the rain till late at night, to visit the beautiful Hôtel de Ville, and other public buildings of that fine old city; and rose early the next morning to see the churches of San Sauveur and Notre Dame, and the magnificent tombs of Charles the Bold and his daughter. Already the churches were crowded with pious Catholics, whose attention was sadly distracted from their devotion by our appearance : sometimes they whispered an Ave Maria with the utmost fervency of prayer ; and sometimes an half-uttered exclamation of wonder burst from their lips ; sometimes they resolutely resumed counting their beads, and sometimes their eyes involuntarily rested on our foreign figures with the broad stare of curiosity.

We left Bruges in the same bark which had once conveyed Napoleon Buonaparte to that city, and which is now used as a côche d'eau. It contained 150 people of every sort and description, from the courtiers of Louis XVIII. down to Flemish peasants; all of whom, however, were obliging, talkative, attentive, flattering, and amusing. After dining on board, and spending a most entertaining day, we arrived in the evening at Ghent.

The whole of Wednesday we spent in this ancient city, and though its extent is so great as to have been the subject of a well-known imperial quibble,* I believe we left but little of it unexplored. We visited its magnificent cathedral, whose walls, pillars, roofs, columns, and pulpits are formed of the richest polished marble of every varying hue, and carved with exquisite skill; and whose sculptured ornaments, the work of ages when the statuary's art was in high perfection, seemed almost to start to life before our eyes. We explored the deep sepulchral gloom of its subterranean church; visited the costly shrines of all the saints; contem-

---

* The Emperor Charles V., in disparagement of the capital City of his rival, used to delight in saying, " Je peux mettre tout Paris dans *mon Gand*." Ghent, on the Continent, is always spelt and pronounced Gand, the same as *gant*, glove.

plated the ancient and decaying monasteries, which were
formerly its pride; made a most indefatigable research after
cabinets of paintings; and wandered with the utmost perseverance through its abominable streets. We saw the balcony
in which the monster Vandamme, in the bloody times of
the Revolution, used to stand, day after day, to see victims
led out, at his bidding, to the guillotine. In its altered
scenes, we now beheld loyal Bourbon beaux in gold epau-
lettes, and smart Flemish belles, in French fashions, laughing
and flirting. We, like them, paraded in its gay promenade,
and rambled through the perfumed walks and exotic bowers
of its beautiful Botanic Garden. The City of Ghent seemed
to be restored to some traces of its ancient grandeur by the
temporary residence of the Bourbon princes, and the little ex-
patriated court of Louis XVIII. I had never been able to
feel any extravagant degree of attachment to this unfortunate
royal family: their restoration had not given me any enthusiastic joy, nor their fall much sorrow; and even the honour
of paying my devoirs to Louis le Désiré, and exchanging some
profound and reverential bows and courtesies with his most
Catholic Majesty, failed to inspire me with much interest or
admiration for this persecuted, princely race. These bows,
by the way, cost the good old king considerable time and
labour, for he is extremely unwieldy and corpulent, and
gouty; and he looks very lethargic and snuffy; and it is
really a thousand pities that an exiled and dethroned monarch should be so remarkably uninteresting a personage.

Early in the morning of Thursday, the 15th of June, we
left the City of Ghent, passed its ancient walls, and crossed
the "lazy Scheldt," which is here but a small stream, and
belies the epithet Goldsmith applies to its more advanced

course; for it runs with considerable rapidity. We proceeded along the straight, undeviating line of the broad, flat chaussée, or paved road, that leads to Brussels. It is bordered on each side with rows of tall trees, which form one long interminable avenue, as far as the eye can reach. We remembered that it was down this very road that Napoleon Buonaparte had made his triumphant progress through the Netherlands, and we most devoutly hoped, that neither by this, nor any other road, he would ever have it in his power to enter them again.

The country is thickly covered with neat cottages, scattered hamlets, and small farm-houses: the fields were waving with tall, luxuriant crops of corn, and far from wearing the appearance of the theatre of war, it seemed to be the abode of peace and plenty; and hope, contentment, and hilarity shone in the countenances of the people. The peasants almost all wore sabots; but the cottage children, bare-footed and bare-headed, frequently pursued the carriage for miles, keeping pace with the horses, tumbling as they went along, singing Flemish patriotic songs, the burden of which was invariably, " Success to the English, and destruction to the French;" and crying with unwearied perseverance, " Vivé* les Anglaises !" " Dat for Napoleon!" expressing at the same time, by an emphatic gesture, cutting off his head. They threw bouquets of flowers into the carriage, twisted their little sunburnt faces into the most extraordinary grimaces, and kept whirling round on their hands and feet, in imitation of the rotatory motion of a wheel. Dr. Clarke, in his Travels, mentions that the children of the Arabs in Egypt performed

* I write it not grammatically, but as they pronounced it, with a strong emphasis on the last letter.

the same exploit, and for the same purpose, that of extorting from the passengers a few sous; nay, even one they seemed to think a sufficient reward for a laborious chase of more than a league, and the exhibition of all these fatiguing antics.

At the little town of Alost, half way to Brussels, we stopped to dine. It was the head-quarters of the Duc de Berri, and the streets, the promenades, and the caffés looked gay. There is a pleasant walk, shaded by trees, round the ramparts; for, this little town, like every other in the Netherlands, was formerly fortified; although its dismantled walls no longer afford any means of defence. A violent shower of rain obliged us to take refuge, in rather an unceremonious manner, in a small house, the mistress of which, who was preparing to take her afternoon's coffee (though it was only one o'clock), received us with the utmost courtesy and kindness. Short as our stay was beneath her roof, it was long enough for her to express with great energy her detestation of Napoleon and of the French; which she said was universal throughout Belgium. We had a good deal of conversation with her upon this subject, and upon the past and present state of Belgium.—" Ah, madame ! before they came among us," she said, " this was a very different country. Then we were rich, and good, and happy." She lamented over the trade, the manufactories, the commerce they had destroyed; the contributions they had exacted; the fine young men they had seized as conscripts; the convents they had ruined; the priests and " les bonnes religieuses" they had turned to the door. Wherever we had gone before, and wherever we afterwards went, we heard the same sentiments from every tongue, and we saw the most unequivocal signs of the inveterate hatred of the Belgic

people towards their former rulers. It bursts out spon-
taneously, as if they could not suppress it; their whole countenances change; their eyes sparkle with indignation; their
very gestures are eloquent, and they seem at a loss for words
strong enough to express the bitterness of their detestation.
This surprised us not a little, as in England we had been
taught to believe that the French were popular in this
country; but we were at length convinced of our mistake.
It is the *English*, not the French, who are popular in Belgium; and it was far more gratifying than any individual
distinction could have been, to find that we were everywhere
received with marked attention and respect for the sake of
our country, and that the name of England is everywhere
beloved and honoured.

At the village of Ashe, half way between Alost and Brussels, while I was buying in a little shop a basket of " gateaux
sucrés," for which the place is famous, two Belgic ladies,
who happened to be there, entered into conversation with
me, with all the ease of foreign manners, and uttered the
same energetic invective against their late French Government, and animated praise of the English, which we heard
from every tongue during our stay in Belgium. These
people evidently speak from their hearts : and yet in manners, in customs, in ancient ties, in modern predilections,
and even in language, they are French. Their deep-rooted
hatred, therefore, of the people to whom they were so firmly
attached, must have sprung from very flagrant wrongs, and
very galling oppression.

Alost is situated on the little river Dender, and from the
road we caught a glimpse of the spire of Dendermond, so
famous for its siege by the Allies in the last century. We

were now in a country which had repeatedly been, in every
age, the seat of war, and in which England had already
gained immortal glory. In retracing the proud history of
her past triumphs, and her recent and not less brilliant con-
quests, we felt the firm assurance that in those scenes where
the British under the Duke of Marlborough had, in the
eighteenth century, won the glorious victories of Oudenarde,
Ramillies, and Malplaquet, the British under the Duke of
Wellington, in the nineteenth century, would gain fresh
laurels and immortal renown, and raise still higher the glory
of their country's arms.

After leaving Alost, the country became more rich and
undulating. Instead of a dull, dead flat, which we had
before traversed, sloping grounds, and distant hills, and
sheltered valleys diversified the prospect. The woods rose
in prouder beauty, and the fields were dressed in brighter
verdure and richer luxuriance; and as we passed through
those smiling scenes, and saw the husbandman pursuing his
peaceful labours, the cottage wife busy with her household
cares, and the merry groups of haymakers spread over the
fragrant meadows, we rejoiced in the hope that the hand of
the spoiler would never lay waste these fruitful fields, nor
burn these peaceful hamlets, and that these contented peasants would never again be torn from their homes to fight
in the cause of unprincipled ambition, and become in turn
the instruments of that oppression of which they had been
the victims. It was with a feeling of pride for our country
we indulged the thought that it was to England they owed
their security; that it was her protecting arm which inter-
posed the impenetrable shield of her armies between them
and the tyranny and usurpation of France. We could not

but rejoice that since the awful struggle must be made, its horrors—if inevitable—would, at least, be distant;—that since the awful thunderbolt of war must fall, it would descend, in all human probability, upon that country which had raised the storm; and that France herself would at length be visited by some part of the dreadful calamities which she had so long and so mercilessly inflicted upon other nations.*

Short sighted mortals! while we fondly indulged these hopes, and exulted in the blessings of security and peace, how little did we suspect that the most aggravated horrors of war were ready to burst over our heads; how little did we foresee the rapid changes and alarming events which even this very day was destined to produce; and while we watched the sun sinking in glory in the western sky, how little did we dream of the scenes that were to pass before the dawn of morning! In all the bliss of ignorance, however, we journeyed along, admiring from afar the lofty towers and spires of Brussels, and its crowded roofs clustering round the steep sides of a hill, in the midst of a rich and cheerful country, and thinking with joyful and impatient anticipation of the well-known faces of the beloved friends whom we were to meet within its walls.

Near Brussels we passed a body of Brunswick troops (called Black Brunswickers). They were dressed in black, and mounted upon black horses, and their helmets were surmounted with tall nodding plumes of black horsehair, which gave them a most sombre and funereal appearance. As they slowly moved along the road before us in a long

* It was not expected at that time that Belgium would be the theatre of war, but that the Allies would advance into France.

regular procession, they looked exactly like an immense
moving hearse. I laughed, and observed to my sister, " that
one might take this for a bad omen, and that it reminded
me of the mourning wedding-ring in the Simple Story."
Some of these black, ominous looking men kept before us,
and entered Brussels along with us. At first we passed
through some mean, dirty streets, but the appearance of the
town soon improved. The houses are large, ancient, and
highly ornamented. There is an air of grandeur and of
architectural design in the towns of Flanders, which is peculiarly striking, on first coming from the plain, diminutive,
shopkeeper-looking, red brick rows of houses in England.
The streets of Brussels are narrow, but they have that air of
bustle, opulence, and animation, which characterises a me-
tropolis. To us everything was new and amusing : the
people, the dresses, the houses, the shops, the very signs
diverted us. Every notice was stuck up in the French language, and quite in the French style : the poorest and most
paltry shop called itself a Magazine. Here were Magasins de
Modes, Magasins de Souliers, Magasins de——everything,
in short : it was amusing to see the names of people and
trades, that we had only been accustomed to meet with in
French books and plays, stuck up in gilt letters above every
shop-door.

Everything wore a military aspect; and the number of
troops of different nations, descriptions, and dresses, which
filled the town, made it look very gay. Soldiers' faces, or
at least their white belts and red coats, were to be seen at
every window ; and in our slow progress through the
streets we were delighted to see the British soldiers, and
particularly the Highlanders, laughing and joking, with

much apparent glee, with the inhabitants. On our right we caught a glimpse of the magnificent spire of the Hôtel de Ville, far exceeding, in architectural beauty, anything I remember to have seen. We slowly continued to ascend the windings of the long and steep hill, which leads from the low to the high town of Brussels, and the upper part of which is called La Montagne du Parc. Passing on our left the venerable towers of the Cathedral, we reached at last the summit of this huge " Montagne ;" and the Parc of Brussels, of which we had heard, read, and talked so much, unexpectedly opened upon us. What a transition from the dark, narrow, gloomy streets of the low town to the lightness, gaiety, and beauty of the Parc, crowded with officers in every variety of military uniform, with elegant women, and with lively parties and gay groups of British and Belgic people, loitering, walking, talking, and sitting under the trees ! There could not be a more animated, a more holiday scene ; everything looked gay and festive, and everything spoke of hope, confidence, and busy expectation.

The Parc of Brussels does not bear the smallest resemblance to what in England we denominate a park. It is more like a garden enclosed with iron rails, the interior of which is laid out with gravel-walks, grass-plots, and parterres, shaded with trees, and ornamented with fountains* and statues. It is quite a promenade, and is exclusively devoted to pedestrians. The walks are formal, but kept with great exactness, and the tout ensemble looks gay, inviting,

* Afterwards, on our return to Brussels, I observed an inscription on one of these fountains, purporting, that the Czar, Peter the Great, having drunk too freely of wine, fell into its waters. The day and year are mentioned. It was, I think, about a century ago.

and pleasant. It is surrounded by a wide street, enclosed by a square of magnificent houses, in which are the palace of the Prince of Orange, and many beautiful public buildings. Compared to this grand square, the finest squares of London, Edinburgh, and Dublin, are small and paltry. Adjoining the Parc is the Place Royale, and so strikingly grand and imposing is its architecture, that we all uttered an involuntary exclamation of surprise and admiration as we drove into it. The doors and windows of the Hôtel Bellevue, and of the Hôtel de Flandre, adjoining to it, were crowded with British officers. We took possession of two pleasant rooms in the latter, which had been secured for us by the kind attention of Sir Neil Campbell. They were in the troisième étage, and we had a hundred steps to ascend; but we were fortunate in procuring such good accommodation, as Brussels was extremely crowded. We had not entered the hotel many minutes, and had not once sat down, when we recognised our pleasant compagnon de voyage, Major Wylie, standing in the Place Royale below, encompassed with officers. He saw us, took off his hat, and, breaking from the people that surrounded him, darted in at the door of the hotel, and was with us in a minute. Breathless with haste, he could scarcely articulate that hostilities had commenced! Our amazement may be conceived: at first we could scarcely believe him to be in earnest. "Upon my honour," exclaimed Major Wylie, still panting, and scarcely able to speak, from the haste with which he had flown up the hundred steps, "it is quite true; and the troops are ordered to be in readiness to march at a moment's notice; and we shall probably leave Brussels to-morrow morning." In answer to our eager inquiries, he then told us that this unexpected intelligence had only just arrived; that he had that moment left the Duke of Wellington's table, where he had been dining with a party of officers ; and that, just as the dessert had been set upon the table, a courier had arrived, bringing dispatches from Marshal Blucher, announcing that he had been attacked by the French: but although the fighting was hot, it seemed to be Blucher's opinion that it would most probably be nothing more than a mere skirmish. While the Duke was reading the dispatches, the Prince of Orange, General Mufflin, and some other foreign officers had come in. After a short debate, the Duke, expecting that the blow would be followed up, and believing that it was the enemy's plan to crush the English army, and take Brussels, immediately ordered the troops to be in readiness to take the field at a moment's notice. "And when did all this happen?— when was this attack made?" we anxiously inquired. "It took place this afternoon." "This afternoon!" I exclaimed, in astonishment, and, I suppose, with looks of consternation, which drew a good-natured smile from Major Wylie, for we had not been used to hear of battles so near, or fought the same afternoon. "Yes, it happened this very afternoon," said Mayor Wylie; "and when the express came away, they were fighting as hard as ever : but after all, it may prove a mere trifling affair of outposts—nothing at all." "But are the French in great force ? Where are they? Where are the Prussians? How far off do you suppose all this fighting is?" were some of the many questions we asked. The fighting was in the neighbourhood of Charleroi, about half a day's march from Brussels : nothing certainly was known of the force of the French. In fact, nothing at all was known, except that the French had this very day attacked the Prussians, when they were totally unprepared, at a short distance from us. "However, after all, this may end in nothing," said Major Wylie, after a pause; "we *may* have to march to-morrow morning, or we may not march these three weeks: but the Duke expects another dispatch from Blucher, and that will settle the business:" and so saying, Major Wylie went away to dress for a ball. Yes, a ball! for the Duke of Wellington, and his aides-de-camp, and half of the British officers, though they expected to go to a battle to-morrow, were going to a ball to-night, at the Duchess of Richmond's; and to the ball they did accordingly go. They seemed to say, or to feel, with the Scottish Chief in Douglas:

> "This night once more
> Within these walls we rest: our tents we pitch
> To-morrow in the field. Prepare the feast!—
> Free is his heart who for his country fights:
> He on the eve of battle may resign
> Himself to social pleasure: sweetest then,
> When danger to a soldier's soul endears
> The human joy that never may return."

Late as it was, my brother and sister went to call upon Mrs. H., whom they were impatient to see. They had not been gone many minutes, when Sir Neil Campbell sent up to ask if I would admit him. I made no objection : so in he came, looking magnificent, in a full dress uniform, covered with crosses, clasps, orders, and medals. Behold me, then, tête-à-tête with this splendid beau, in my own room, between ten and eleven o'clock at night! In England it would have been extraordinary enough, to be sure; but in Brussels it was nothing. It was impossible to receive him, or anybody else, in any other place than a bed-room, for the Hôtel de Flandre was entirely composed of bed-rooms, all of which were occupied. Without discomposing myself about the matter, therefore, I gave Sir Neil Campbell some tea, and we had a long chat together. He, too, had been dining with the Duke of Wellington, and had been present when these important dispatches arrived, and from him I heard a repetition of all that Major Wylie had told us, with the alarming addition, that the French were said to be upwards of 100,000 strong, and that Napoleon himself was at the head of the army. It was generally thought that this attack upon the Prussians was a stratagem to conceal more effectually his real designs, of surprising Brussels, and destroying, if possible, at one blow, the English army. It was well known that the Russians had crossed the Rhine; and Sir Neil Campbell said *he* had no doubt that Buonaparte would push forward at all hazards, and give battle before they could arrive. As Sir Neil Campbell had certainly reason to know *something* of Buonaparte, and as these rapid, unexpected movements were in perfect uniformity with his general policy, this conjecture seemed but too probable; but we concluded that the numbers of the French must be prodigiously exaggerated. It seemed quite incredible that so large an army could have formed, advanced, and even attacked Marshal Blucher, without his having any knowledge of their movements; and even if their force was very superior to ours, I felt confident that they would meet with a very different reception from that which they expected; and that Napoleon, with every advantage on his side, would not find the defeat of an English army quite so easy a thing in practice, as he had always seemed to consider it in theory. Having settled this point much to our mutual satisfaction, Sir Neil Campbell went away. My brother and sister returned, and we went to bed.

But we were not destined long to enjoy the sweets of repose. Scarcely had I laid my weary head on the pillow,
when the bugle's loud and commanding call sounded from
the Place Royale. " Is that the call to arms?" I exclaimed,
starting up in the bed. My sister laughed at the idea; but
it was repeated, and we listened with eager and anxious
suspense. For a few moments a pause of doubt ensued. Hark!
again! it sounded through the silence of the night, and
from every quarter of the town it was now repeated, at
short and regular intervals. " It is the call to arms!" I exclaimed. Instantly the drums beat; the Highland pibroch
sounded——It was the call to arms! Oh! never shall I
forget the feelings of that moment! Immediately the utmost tumult and confusion succeeded to the silence in which
the city had previously been buried. At half-past two we
were roused by a loud knocking at our room door, and my
brother's voice calling to us to get up instantly, not to lose a
moment—that the troops were under arms—were marching
out against the French—and that Major Llewellyn was waiting to see us before he left Brussels. Inexpressibly relieved
to find that this nocturnal alarm was occasioned by the departure of Major Llewellyn, not by the arrival of the French,
which, in the first startling confusion of my thoughts, and
trepidation of my mind, had actually entered my head; and
much better pleased to meet an old and kind friend, than to
run away from a furious enemy, we got up with the greatest
alacrity, and hastily throwing some clothes about us, flew to
see Llewellyn, who was waiting on the stairs. Short and
agitated indeed was our meeting under such circumstances.
By the light of a candle in my brother's room, we sat down
for a few minutes on some boxes, scarcely able to believe our

senses, that all this was real, and almost inclined to doubt whether it was not a dream: but the din of war which resounded in our ears too painfully convinced us that it was no illusion of phantasy:—we could scarcely even " snatch a fearful joy," for not for a single moment could we banish from our minds the impression, that in a few moments we must part, perhaps for ever, and that this hurried interview might prove our last. We could only gaze intently upon each other, as if to retain a lasting remembrance of the well-known countenance, should we indeed be destined to meet no more: we could only utter incoherent words or disjointed speeches. While he still lingered, we heard his charger, which his servant held in the court-yard below, neighing and pawing the ground, as if impatient of his master's delay, and eager to bear him to the field. Our greetings and adieus were equally hurried. We bade him farewell, and saw him go to battle.

It was nearly two years since we had met; and little did we think, when we parted in the peaceful valleys of Roxburghshire, that our next, and perhaps our last, meeting would be in Brussels, in the dead of the night, and on the very eve of battle. He was the same to us as a brother. He left us then, as now, to fight the battles of his country; and we trusted that victory and glory would still follow the British arms, and that he would once more return in honour and safety.

Just as he left us, the dawn appeared, and, by the faint twilight of morning, we saw the Place Royale filled with armed men, and with all the tumult and confusion of marsial preparation. All was " hurry skurry for the field. Officers were looking in vain for their servants—servants running in pursuit of their masters—baggage waggons were loading—bât horses preparing—trains of artillery harnessing.—And amidst the clanking of horses' hoofs, the rolling of heavy carriages, the clang of arms, the sounding of bugles, and the neighing of chargers, we distinctly heard, from time to time, the loud, deep-toned word of command, while the incessant din of hammers nailing " gave dreadful note of preparation."

A second express had arrived from Blucher, bringing intelligence that the French were in much more formidable force than he had imagined ; that the attack was become serious; they had taken Charleroi, and driven back the Prussians. It was, therefore, necessary for the British to march immediately to support them. The Duke had received the dispatches containing this important news in the ball-room. We were afterwards told, that upon perusing them he seemed for a few minutes to be absolutely absorbed in a profound reverie, and completely abstracted from every surrounding object; and that he was even heard to utter indistinctly a few words to himself. After a pause, he folded up the dispatches, called one of his staff officers to him, gave the necessary orders with the utmost coolness and promptitude; and having directed the army to be put in motion immediately, he himself stayed at the ball till past two in the morning. The cavalry officers, whose regiments, for the most part, were quartered in villages about the frontier, ten, fifteen, and even twenty miles off, flew from the ball-room in dismay, in search of their horses, and galloped off in the dark, without baggage or attendants, in the utmost perplexity which way to go, or where to join their regiments, which might have marched before they could arrive.

Numbers of the officers had·been out when the first order to be in readiness to march was issued, and remained in perfect ignorance of the commencement of hostilities, until the alarm sounded, and called them from scenes of festivity and mirth to scenes of war and bloodshed. As the dawn broke, the soldiers were seen assembling from all parts of the town, in marching order, with their knapsacks on their backs, loaded with three days' provision. Unconcerned in the midst of the din of war, many a soldier laid himself down on a truss of straw, and soundly slept, with his hands still grasping his firelock; others were sitting contentedly on the pavement, waiting the arrival of their comrades. Numbers were taking leave of their wives and children, perhaps for the last time, and many a veteran's rough cheek was wet with the tears of sorrow. One poor fellow, immediately under our windows, turned back again and again, to bid his wife farewell, and take his baby once more in his arms; and I saw him hastily brush away a tear with the sleeve of his coat, as he gave her back the child for the last time, wrung her hand, and ran off to join his company, which was drawn up on the other side of the Place Royale.

Many of the soldiers' wives marched out with their husbands to the field, and I saw one young English lady mounted on horseback, slowly riding out of town along with an officer, who, no doubt, was her husband. But even at this interesting moment, when thousands were parting with those nearest and dearest to their hearts, my gravity was suddenly overset, and my sorrow turned into mirth, by the unexpected appearance of a long train of market carts, loaded with cabbages, green peas, cauliflowers, early potatoes, old women, and strawberries, peaceably jog-

ging along, one after another, to market. These good
people, who had never heard of battles, and who were perfectly at a loss to comprehend what could be the meaning
of all this uproar, stared with astonishment at the spectacle
before them, and actually gaped with wonder, as they slowly
made their way in their long carts through the crowds of
soldiers which filled the Place Royale. There was something so inexpressibly ludicrous in the contrast which the
grotesque figures and rustic dresses of these old women
presented to this martial hurry and confusion, that really
"*not* to laugh surpassed all powers of face," and that I did
laugh I must acknowledge, though it was perhaps very ill-
timed levity. Soon afterwards the 42nd and 92nd Highland regiments marched through the Place Royale and the
Parc, with their bagpipes playing before them, while the
bright beams of the rising sun shone full on their polished
muskets, and on the dark waving plumes of their tartan
bonnets. We admired their fine athletic forms, their firm
erect military demeanour and undaunted mien. We felt
proud that they were our countrymen: in their gallant
bearing we recognised the true hardy sons of Caledon, men
who would conquer or die ; and we could not restrain a tear
at the reflection, how few of that warlike band who now
marched out so proudly to battle might ever live to return.
Alas! we little thought that even before the fall of night
these brave men, whom we now gazed at with so much
interest and admiration, would be laid low!

During the whole night, or rather morning, we stood at
the open window, unable to leave these sights and sounds of
war, or to desist for a moment from contemplating a scene
so new, so affecting, and so deeply interesting to us. Regi-

ment after regiment formed and marched out of Brussels; we heard the last word of command—March! the heavy measured uniform tread of the soldiers' feet upon the pavement, and the last expiring note of the bugles, as they sounded from afar.

We saw our gallant army leave Brussels with emotions which may be better imagined than described.   They went again to meet that enemy whom they had so often encountered, and as invariably vanquished ; to follow that general, who, in a long course of years of command devoted to the service and glory of his country, had never experienced a single defeat ; who had so lately led them from victory to victory, crossed, in his triumphant march, the plains of Spain, fought his way over the frozen heights of the Pyrenees, carried conquest and dismay in the very heart of France, and whose rapid and unparalleled career of conquest had only been checked by the angel of peace.   As we saw the last of our brave troops march out of Brussels, the recollection of their past glory, the proud hopes of their present triumph, the greatness of the contest, upon the issue of which the fate of Europe and the security of the world depended ; the dread of their encounter with the numerous and formidable hosts of *that man*, whom no treaties could bind, no adversity could amend, no considerations of justice or humanity could soften, no laws, divine or human, could restrain, swelled our hearts with feelings which language is too feeble to express: and our brave countrymen were followed by our tears, our warmest wishes, and our most fervent prayers for their safety and success.

Before seven in the morning, the streets, which had been so lately thronged with armed men and with busy crowds, were empty and silent.   The great square of the Place

Royale no longer resounded with the tumult and preparations for war. The army were gone, and Brussels seemed a perfect desert. The mourners they had left behind were shut up in their solitary chambers, and the faces of the few who were slowly wandering about the streets were marked with the deepest anxiety and melancholy. The heavy military waggons, ranged in order, and ready to move as occasion might require, were standing under the silent guard of a few sentinels. The Flemish drivers were sleeping in the long tilted carts destined to convey the wounded; and the horses, ready to harness at a moment's notice, were quietly feeding on fresh-cut grass by their side: the whole livelong day and night did these Flemish men and horses pass in the Place Royale. A few officers were still to be seen, slowly riding out of town to join the army. The Duke of Wellington set off about eight o'clock, in great spirits, declaring he expected to be back by dinner-time; and dinner was accordingly prepared for him. Sir Thomas Picton, who, like ourselves, had only arrived in Brussels the day before, rode through the streets in true soldier-like style, with his reconnoitring glass slung across his shoulders, reining in his charger as he passed, to exchange salutations with his friends, and left Brussels—never to return.

We had a most agreeable surprise at our breakfast-table in the sight of Major Llewellyn. He had ridden a few miles out of Brussels with the regiment, and then galloped back with Sir Philip Belson, who also wished to return. We spent a few hours together, and, embittered as they were with the prospect of so near and dreadful a separation, there was much consolation in thus meeting. No expectation was entertained of any engagement taking place to-day. Sir

Philip Belson and Major Llewellyn, therefore, felt quite at
their ease; " being certain," they said, " of overtaking the
regiment *at a place called Waterloo*, where the men were
to stop to cook." Little did any of us then suspect how memorable to future ages " that place called Waterloo" was
destined to become! We denied ourselves to several idlers,
but Sir Neil Campbell, and Mr. and Mrs. H., succeeded in
gaining admittance.

At last the moment of parting arrived; Sir Philip Belson
called for Major Llewellyn, and, after sitting a few moments,
they got up to go away, and we bade farewell to one who
from childhood had been our friend and companion, and
whom we loved as another brother. We could not but feel
how probable it was that we might never see him more;
and, under this impression, some minutes after he had left
us, which he had spent in bidding farewell to my brother
below, we ran to the window, saw Sir Philip Belson and
him mount their horses and ride away, and caught the last
glimpse of them as they passed under the gateway of the
Place Royale. Two hours afterwards they were in the
thickest of the battle!

Although we had not the smallest suspicion that any engagement could take place to-day, our anxiety for news,
both of the French and Prussians, was extreme; but we
could hear nothing but vague, unauthenticated reports,
upon which no reliance could be placed.

We dined, or rather sat down to dinner, at the table
d'hôte, and afterwards wandered restlessly about the streets,
our minds too much absorbed in the approaching contest, to
see, hear, understand, think, or talk about anything but what
related to public events.

Our consternation may be imagined when we were told that a dreadful cannonade had been heard from the Parc, in the very direction which our army had taken, and that it was supposed they must have been attacked by the French within a few miles of Brussels. At first I was utterly incredulous; I could not, would not believe it; but, hurrying to the Parc, we were too soon, too incontestably convinced of the dreadful truth, by ourselves hearing the awful and almost incessant thunder of the guns apparently very near to us. For many hours this tremendous cannonade continued, while, unable to gain any intelligence of what was passing, ignorant of everything, except of the fact, proclaimed by the loud and repeated voice of war, that there was a battle, we listened in a state of terrible uncertainty and suspense, and thought with horror, in the roar of every cannon, that our brave countrymen were every moment falling in agony and death.

Unable to rest, we wandered about, and lingered till a late hour in the Parc. The Parc! what a different scene did its green alleys present this evening from that which they exhibited at the same hour last night! Then it was crowded with the young and the gay, and the gallant of the British army, with the very men who were now engaged in deadly strife, and perhaps bleeding on the ground. Then it was filled with female faces sparkling with mirth and gaiety; now terror, and anxiety, and grief were marked upon every countenance we met.

In addition to the general alarm and anxiety, which surpassed anything it is in my power to describe, we had a particular subject of solicitude. We had but too much reason to fear that it would be impossible for Sir Philip Belson and

Major Llewellyn to join their regiment in time for the action. The idea, the very doubt was dreadful. If *we* listened to the cannonade with such heart-sinking apprehensions for them, what must have been *their* feelings, if, at a distance from the army, absent without leave, they heard its sounds! After years of service in various climates and countries, after six long and glorious campaigns in the Peninsula, would they forfeit, by one act of imprudence, all the distinction they had obtained by a life devoted to their country, and be found absent from their post in the hour of danger! Dear to us as was the life of our friend, his honour was still dearer; and while every one else was anxiously dreading lest the battle should be near, and trembling at the reports that prevailed of its vicinity, I was secretly praying that it might not be distant, and would have felt inexpressibly relieved to have been assured that it was within a few miles of Brussels.

But it was in vain we attempted to discover where it really was. Some people said it was only six, some that it was ten, and some that it was twenty miles off. Numbers of people in carriages and on horseback had gone out several miles on the road which the army had taken, and all of them had come back in perfect ignorance of the real circumstances of the case, and with some ridiculous report, which, for a time, was circulated as the truth. No authentic intelligence could be gained; and every minute we were assailed with the most absurd and contradictory stories. One moment we heard that the allied army had obtained a complete victory; that the French had been completely repulsed, and had left *twenty thousand dead* upon the field of battle. Gladly would I have believed the first part of this story, but the *twenty thousand dead* I could not swallow. Then again we were told that the French, 180,000 strong, had attacked the British, that the Belgians had abandoned their arms and fled, that our troops were literally cut to pieces, and that the French were advancing to Brussels. Then an English gentleman stopped his carriage to tell us, that *he* had been out farther than anybody, and that he had actually *seen* the engagement, which was between the French and the Prussians, and that old Blucher had given the rascals a complete beating. We had not gone ten paces farther, before another man, in a great hurry, advised us to set off instantly if we wished to make our escape; that he was on the point of going, for that certain intelligence had been received " that the French had won the battle, and that our army was retreating in the utmost confusion." I never remember to have felt so angry in my life; and I indignantly exclaimed, that such a report deserved only to be treated with contempt, and that it must be false, for that the English would never retreat *in confusion.* The man seemed a little ashamed of himself, and Mr. H. advised him "by all means to take care of himself, and set off directly." We hastened on. Presently we met another of Mr. H.'s wise friends, who assured us, with a face of the greatest solemnity, " that the day was going against us; that the battle was as good as lost; that our troops had been driven back from one position after another; and that the artillery and baggage had commenced the retreat; that all the horses would be seized for the service of the army; and that in two hours it would be impossible to get away." All this time we could hear nothing of what was really passing; or these idle tales and unfounded rumours were unworthy of a moment's attention, and did not give us a moment's alarm; but the poor Belgians, not knowing what to make of all this, and nearly frightened out of their senses, firmly expected the French in Brussels before the morning; for their terror of them was so great and so deeply rooted, that they believed nothing on earth could stop their advance.

This dreadful uncertainty and ignorance of the truth made us truly wretched. Nobody knew anything of the actual state of affairs. Nobody could tell where our army was engaged, nor under what circumstances, nor against what force, nor whether separately or conjointly with the Prussians, nor which side was gaining the advantage. We knew nothing, except that there was a battle, and that at no great distance from us; for that the unceasing cannonade too certainly proved. Anxiously and vainly we looked for news from the army—none arrived. The consternation of the people was not to be described. "The cannonade is approaching nearer!" they exclaimed. "Hark! how loud was that peal! There, again! Our army must be retreating. Good heavens! what will become of us!" On every side, in the tones of terror and despondency, we heard these exclamations repeated. Heard through the density and stillness of the evening air, the cannonade did, in fact, seem to approach nearer, and become more tremendous. During the whole evening we wandered about the Parc, or stood in silence on the ramparts, listening to the dreadful thunder of the battle. At length it became less frequent. How often did we hope it had ceased, and vainly flatter ourselves that each peal was the last! when, again, after an awful pause, a louder, a longer roar burst on our ears, and it raged more tremendously than ever. To our great relief, about half-past nine, it became fainter and fainter, and at last entirely died away.

After we had returned to the hotel, Sir Neil Campbell, who, in our absence, had been twice at our rooms and in the Parc in search of us, good-naturedly came again, to tell us that he had met Sir G. Scovell, who had left the field with orders from Brussels about half-past five, and that so far " all was well." The French army had encountered our troops on their march, upon the high road, about fifteen miles from Brussels. The 92nd and 42nd Highland regiments were the first in order of march. These brave men immediately made a stand, formed into squares, received the furious onset of the French with undaunted intrepidity, and alone sustained the fight, until the Royal Scots, the 28th, and some other regiments, came up to support them. Every regiment, as it arrived, instantly formed and fought ; and though the English had been taken by surprise, unprepared, unconcentrated ; without cavalry, and with scarcely any artillery; and, though the enemy outnumbered them far beyond all computation, they had not yielded an inch of ground, and they were still fighting in the fullest confidence of success. " There can be no doubt of their repulsing the French," said Colonel Scovell, " but nothing of any importance can be done till the cavalry come up, which it is expected they will do this evening. To-morrow the engagement will most probably be renewed, and I hope it will prove decisive." The Duke, he said, who was in excellent spirits, was to sleep to-night at Genappe.

Certainly no other troops but the English, without any cavalry, and with very little artillery, would have thought themselves sure of repulsing an enemy with both, and with an almost countless superiority of numbers: and most certainly none but the English could have achieved it. It is a perversion of words to call the troops engaged in the battle of Quatre Bras the English army. During the greater part of the day a few regiments only, a mere handful of men, were opposed to the immense masses the French continually poured down against them; but they formed impenetrable squares, which were in vain attacked by the French cavalry, "steel-clad cuirassiers," and infantry; and against which tremendous showers of shot and shell descended in vain.

The 92nd, 42nd, 79th, the 28th, the 95th, and the Royal Scots, were the first, and most hotly, engaged.* For several hours these brave troops alone maintained the tremendous onset, and the shock of the whole French army, and to their determined valour Belgium owes her independence, and England her glory. I do not, however, mean to give them exclusive praise. I do not doubt that had the post of honour fallen upon other British regiments, they would have acquitted themselves equally well: but let honour be paid where it is so justly due. Let England be sensible of the vast debt of gratitude she owes them; and let the names of those who perished there be enrolled in the long list of her noblest heroes! The 92nd, 42nd, and 79th Highland regiments had suffered most severely. They had received the furious and combined attack of the French cavalry and infantry, from first to last, with undaunted firmness, till, after supporting this unequal contest the whole day, after making immense havoc among their columns, and repeatedly charging and driving them back in confusion, they had themselves fallen, overpowered by numbers, and among heaps of

* [The 32nd and 44th should be added.—ED.]

the slaughtered enemy, on the very spot where they first stood to arms; and we were told that they were, almost to a man, cut to pieces. With grief and horror, not to be described, we thought of these gallant soldiers whom, in the morning, we had seen march out so proudly to battle, and who were now lying insensible in death on the plains of Quatre Bras. They had fought, and they had fallen, as became the same noble spirits who had wrested from the same vaunting foe the standard of the Invincibles on the sands of Egypt. They were gallantly supported by the 28th, who, on the same soil, as well as in the long campaigns of Spain, had gained immortal honour, and who particularly distinguished themselves in this day's battle by their complete repulse of the French cuirassiers, who, though clad in mail, and "armed at all points precisely cap-à-pie," were driven back with immense loss from every attack, and uniformly gave way before the dreaded British charge with the bayonet. One regiment of raw Belgic troops had turned and fled where they had the finest opportunity of charging. I confess I was not sorry to hear that these recreant Belgians had, almost to a man, been cut to pieces by the very French troops they had not courage to face. The fate of cowards is unpitied. The consequences of their misconduct had, however, been retrieved by part of Sir Thomas Picton's division,* which regained the post they had lost, though with considerable slaughter.

After hearing this account our spirits completely revived, I

---

* Consisting of the 28th, 32nd, 79th, 95th, a battalion of the 1st, or Royal Scots, the 42nd, 92nd, and the 2nd battalion of the 44th, and a battalion of Hanoverians. It was the first division which arrived, and, during the principal part of the day, it was the only part of the British army engaged.

scarcely knew why; for, except in the new proof we had just had of invincible British valour and firmness, there was nothing to inspire satisfaction or confidence. We had just learned, beyond all doubt, the truth of the alarming report, that the Prussians were separately engaged with another division of the enemy, which completely outnumbered them. Thus the allied armies seemed to be effectually cut off, and prevented from assisting each other, or acting in concert. The French then, whose combined numbers report magnified to 180,000, were on two sides of us, at the distance of only three hours' march from Brussels. Their army was collected, combined, concentrated, and well-appointed. The Prussians and the English were surprised, separated, dispersed, and unprepared ; the latter were destitute of cavalry, ill-supported by artillery, and with an appalling inferiority even of infantry; and these too partly composed of Belgians, who seemed to make a practice of running away. Yet, in spite of all these disadvantages, they *had* bravely stood the first brunt of the battle, and we felt the firm assurance that they would eventually triumph.

Colonel Scovell had left the army at half-past five ; the battle, or at least the cannonading, had lasted till about ten; and our anxiety to know its results, our impatience for further news from the army, may be imagined ; but no later intelligence arrived; we could hear nothing but vague reports of defeat, disaster, and dismay, to which, as they were founded upon no authority, we paid no attention. Sir Neil Campbell was going to join the army, like many others who had no business there:—he was to set off at one in the morning, so that we should see him no more, and what was infinitely worse, receive no more, through him, immediate and au-

D

thentic intelligence of all that was known. In this respect he
was a great loss to us; for he was indefatigable in bringing us
news, and took unwearied pains to be of use to us in every
possible way.

Late as it was we went to see Mrs. H., whom we knew
to be in great alarm. We found her sitting surrounded by
plate, which she was vainly trying to acquire sufficient composure to pack up, with a face pale with consternation, and
quite overcome with agitation and distress. We did all we
could to assist, and said all we could to console and reassure
her. Mr. H. had gone out towards the army, and, late as it
was, had not yet returned. We stayed with her some time,
and had the satisfaction of leaving her in much better spirits
than we found her.

My brother had engaged, and made an agreement to pay
for, horses, upon the condition of their being in readiness
to convey us to Antwerp at a moment's warning, by day or
night, if required. We had not, however, the smallest intention of leaving Brussels for some days to come, unless some
sudden and unexpected change in public events should render
it absolutely necessary. Thinking it, however, prudent to
be prepared, we had sent our valet de place to la blanchisseuse to desire her to send home everything belonging to
us early in the morning. La blanchisseuse sent back a
message literally to this effect,—" Madame," said the valet,
addressing himself to me in French, " the blanchisseuse says,
that if the English should beat the French, she will iron
and plait your clothes, and finish them for you ; but if, au
contraire, these vile French should get the better, then she
will assuredly send them all back quite wet—tout mouillé—
early to-morrow morning." At this speech, which the valet

delivered with immoveable gravity, we all, with one accord, burst out a laughing, irresistibly amused to find that amongst the important consequences of Buonaparte's gaining the victory, would be our clothes remaining unplaited and un-ironed ; and that the British were, in a manner, fighting, in order that the getting up of our fine linen might be properly performed. The valet, as soon as he could obtain a hearing, went on to say, that he sincerely hoped we should get our clothes dried and finished, and that the English would beat " ces diables de Français ;" but this seemed quite a secondary consideration with the valet, compared with ironing our clothes, and we were again seized with an uncontrollable fit of laughter. Even the valet's long face of dismay relaxed into something like a smile, and, as he left the room, he said to himself, " Mais ces demoiselles sont bien enjouées."

It was half-past twelve ; and hopeless now of hearing any further news from the army, we were preparing to retire to rest—but rest was a blessing we were not destined to enjoy in Brussels. We were suddenly startled by the sound of the rapid rolling of heavy military carriages passing at full speed through the Place Royale :—a great tumult instantly took place among the people below ; the baggage waggons, which we knew were not to set off, except in a case of emergency, were harnessed in an instant, and the noise and tumult be-came every instant more alarming. For some minutes we listened in silence : faster and faster, and louder and louder, the long train of artillery continued to roll through the town: —the cries of the affrighted people increased. I hastily flew out to inquire the cause of this violent commotion. The first person I encountered was a poor, scared fille de chambre, nearly frightened out of her wits. " Ah, madame!" she

exclaimed, " les François sont tout près ; dans une petite
demi-heure ils seront ici.—Ah, grand Dieu! Ah, Jésus!
Jésus! que ferons - nous! que ferons - nous!" In vain I
eagerly asked how she knew, or why she believed, or from
whence this news came, that the French were near ? She
could only reiterate, again and again, " Les François sont
tout près—les François sont tout près!" my questions were
unanswered and unheard ; but suddenly recollecting herself,
she earnestly besought us to set off instantly, exclaiming,
" Mais, mesdames, vous êtes Anglaises—il faut partir tout de
suite—*tout de suite*," she repeated, with great emphasis and
gesticulation, and then resumed her exclamations and lamentations.

As I flew down stairs the house seemed deserted. The
doors of the rooms (which in foreign hotels are not only shut,
but locked) were all wide open ; the candles were burning
upon the tables, and the solitude and silence which reigned
in the house formed a fearful contrast to the increasing tumult without. At the bottom of the staircase a group of
affrighted Belgians were assembled, all crowding and talking
together with Belgic volubility. They cried out that news
had arrived of the battle having terminated in the defeat of
the British ; that all the artillery and baggage of the army
were retreating ; and that a party of Belgians had just entered the town, bringing intelligence that a large body of
French had been seen advancing through the woods to
take Brussels, and that they were only two leagues off. In
answer to my doubts and my questions, they all exclaimed,
" Ah! c'est trop vrai; c'est trop vrai. Ne restez pas ici,
mademoiselle, ne restez pas ici; partez, éloignez vous vîte:
c'est affreux !"

"Mais demain matin——" I began.

"Ah! demain matin," eagerly interrupted a little good-humoured Belgic woman belonging to the hotel—"demain matin il n'y aura pas plus le tems—une autre heure peut-être, et il ne sera pas plus possible de partir." "Ecoutez, mademoiselle, écoutez!" they cried, turning paler and paler as the thundering noise of the artillery increased. At this moment several people, among whom were some English gentlemen and servants, rushed past us to the stables, calling for their carriages to be got ready instantly. "Apprêtes les chevaux, tout de suite—Vite! vite! il n'a pas un moment!" was loudly repeated in all the hurry of fear. These people confirmed the alarm. I sent for our côcher, and most reluctantly we began to think that we must set off; when we found, to our inexpressible joy, that the long trains of artillery, which still continued to roll past with the noise of thunder, were not flying from the army, but advancing to join it. It is impossible to conceive the blessed relief this intelligence gave us. From that moment we felt assured that the army was safe, and our fears for ourselves were at an end. My brother, who had been roused from his sleep, and who, like many other people, had been running about half-dressed, and was still standing in his nightcap, in much perplexity what to do, now went to bed again with great joy, declaring he was resolved to disturb himself no more about these foolish alarms.

We were now perfectly incredulous as to the whole story of the French having been seen advancing through the woods to take Brussels; but the Belgians still remained convinced of it; and though they differed about how it would be done, they all agreed that Brussels would be taken.

Some of them said that the British, and some that the Prussians, had been defeated, and some that both of them had been defeated, and that the French, having broken through their lines, were advancing to take Brussels; others believed that Buonaparte, while he kept the allies employed, had sent round a detachment, under cover of night, by a circuitous route, to surprise the town ; but it seemed to be the general opinion, that before morning the French would be here. The town was wholly undefended, either by troops or fortifications; it was well known to be Napoleon's great object to get possession of it, and that he would leave no means untried to effect it. The battle had been fought against the most fearful disparity of numbers, and under the most disadvantageous circumstances to the British. Its event still remained unknown ; above all, no intelligence from our army had arrived. Under such circumstances it was not surprising that the general despondency should be so great ; while continual rumours of defeat, disaster, and dismay, and incessant alarms, only served to confirm their worst fears. As the French, however, had not yet come, this panic in some degree subsided, and comparative quietness seemed to be restored. Great alarm, however, continued to prevail through the whole night, and the baggage waggons stood ready harnessed to set off at a moment's notice. Several persons took their departure, but we quietly went to bed. My sister, however, only lay down in her clothes, observing, half in jest, and half in earnest, that we might, perhaps, be awakened by the entrance of the French ; and overcome with fatigue, we both fell fast asleep. Her prediction seemed to be actually verified, for at six o'clock we were roused by a violent knocking at the room-door, accompanied by the

cries of "Les François sont ici! les François sont ici!"
Starting out of bed, the first sight we beheld from the window was a troop of Belgic cavalry galloping from the army
at the most furious rate, through the Place Royale, as if the
French were at their heels ; and instantly the whole train of
baggage waggons and empty carts, which had stood before
our eyes so long, set off, full speed, by the Montagne de la
Cour, and through every street by which it was possible to
effect their escape. In an instant the whole great square of
the Place Royale, which had been crowded with men,
horses, carts, and carriages, was completely cleared, as if by
magic, and entirely deserted. The terrified people fled in
every direction, as if for their lives. While my sister, who
had never undressed, flew to rouse my brother, and I threw
on my clothes I scarcely knew how ; I heard again the
dreadful cries of "Les François sont ici ! Ils s'emparent de
la porte de la ville !" My toilet, I am quite certain, did not
occupy one minute ; and as I flew down stairs, in the hope
that it might yet be possible to effect our escape, I met
numbers of bewildered-looking people running about half-
dressed in every direction, in all the distraction of fear. The
men with their nightcaps on, and half their clothes under
their arms; the women with their dishevelled hair hanging
about their shoulders, and all of them pale as death, and
trembling in every limb. Some were flying down stairs
loaded with all sorts of packages ; others running up to the
garrets sinking under the accumulated weight of the most
heterogeneous articles. The poor fille de chambre, nearly
frightened out of her senses, was standing half-way down
the stairs, wringing her hands, and unable to articulate
anything but "Les François ! les François !" A little

lower, another woman was crying bitterly, and exclaimed, as I passed her, "Nous sommes tous perdus!" But no language can do justice to the scene of confusion which the court below exhibited : masters and servants, ladies and stable-boys, valets and soldiers, lords and beggars; Dutchmen, Belgians, and Britons; bewildered garçons and scared filles de chambre ; enraged gentlemen and clamorous coachmen ; all crowded together, jostling, crying, scolding, squabbling, lamenting, exclaiming, imploring, swearing, and vociferating, in French, English, and Flemish, all at the same time. Nor was it only a war of words ; the disputants had speedily recourse to blows, and those who could not get horses by fair means endeavoured to obtain them by foul. The unresisting animals were dragged away half-harnessed. The carriages were seized by force, and jammed against each other. Amidst the crash of wheels, the volleys of oaths, and the confusion of tongues, the mistress of the hotel, with a countenance dressed in woe, was carrying off her most valuable plate in order to secure it, ejaculating, as she went, the name of Jesus incessantly, and, I believe, unconsciously; while the master, with a red nightcap on his head, and the eternal pipe sticking mechanically out of one corner of his mouth, was standing with his hands in his pockets, a silent statue of despair.

Amidst this uproar I soon found out our côcher, but, to my utter consternation, he vehemently swore, "that he would neither go himself, nor let his horses go ; no, not to save the King of Holland himself; for that the French were just at hand, and that they would take his horses, and murder him :" and neither entreaties, nor bribes, nor arguments, nor persuasions, had the smallest effect upon him ;

he remained inexorable, and so did numbers of the fraternity. While my brother, who had now come down stairs, was vainly and angrily expostulating with him, I inquired on all sides, and of all people, if there was no possibility of procuring other horses. The good-natured garçon of the house exclaimed, " That if there were horses to be had in Brussels, I should have them ;" and away he ran in quest of them, while I continued my fruitless inquiries. In a little while he returned disappointed and unsuccessful, exclaiming, with a face of horror that I shall never forget, " Il n'y a pas un seul cheval, et les François sont tout près de la ville." At this moment in rushed Mr. H., in an agony of terror, panting, breathless, and exhausted, crying to us " that his carriage was ready, that they could carry one of us, and that we must come away instantly." It was to no purpose both he and I implored my sister to accompany them, but she was inflexible. Nothing could induce her to go without us, and, finding she was immoveable, Mr. H. ran off with the good-natured intention of taking Lady W., since we refused to go singly. With incredible expedition, one English carriage after another drove off at full speed, and we were left to our fate. Of the rapid approach of the enemy we could not entertain the smallest doubt. To say I was frightened is nothing : I honestly confess I never knew what terror was before. Never shall I forget the horror of those moments. Our own immediate danger, and all the dreadful list of uncertain, undefined evils to which we might be exposed, in the power of those merciless savages ; the anxiety, the distress, and despair of our friends at home, joined to the dreadful idea that the English army had been overwhelmed by numbers, defeated, perhaps cut to pieces, agonised my mind with feelings which it is impossible to describe. Escape seemed, however, impossible: like Richard, I would have gladly given my kingdom (if I had had one) for a horse, or at least for a pair; but no horses were to be had, neither for love, money, nor kingdoms.

In the midst of this state of terror and suspense, I suddenly beheld Major Wylie. If an angel had descended from heaven I could not have welcomed him with more transport. Hope revived: and, springing forward to meet him, I exclaimed: "Oh! Major Wylie, is it true?" His countenance inspired little comfort; he looked pale, and struck with horror and consternation. "God forbid!" he exclaimed: "I hope not. I do not believe it; but I am going to inquire, and I will come back to you immediately." He wrung my hand, and hurried away. In the mean time I flew up-stairs to collect all our things, and bundle them together, to be ready for instant departure, if we should be able to procure horses. Never was packing more expeditiously performed: I am certain it did not occupy anything like three minutes. With the help of the valet de place, I crammed them all together, wet and dry, into the travelling-bags, trunks, and portmanteaus, without the smallest ceremony.

Every minute seemed to be an age, till at last Major Wylie returned with the blessed assurance that it was a false alarm; "that for the present, at least, we were in no danger." It is quite impossible to give the smallest idea of the transport we felt when we found that the enemy were not at hand, that our army was not defeated, and that we ourselves were not in the power of the French. I never can forget the ecstasy of that moment—the bliss of that deliverance, and the inexpressible comfort of those feelings of safety which we now enjoyed. No fabled spirit, emerging from the dark and dismal regions of Pluto to the brightness and beauty of the Elysian Fields, could feel more transporting joy than we did when "the spectre forms of terror" fled, and we felt secure from every danger. From two English gentlemen, and lastly from Lord C., we received a confirmation of these happy tidings. The alarm had been raised by those dastardly Belgians whom we had seen scampering through the town, and who had most probably been terrified by the same foraging party of the enemy which, as we were afterwards told, had come up even to the gates of the city, insolently summoning it to surrender. They were supposed to have come from the side of the Prussians; and, knowing the defenceless state of Brussels, amused themselves with this bravado. Their appearance had confirmed the alarm beyond all doubt, and given rise to the dreadful cry that the French were seizing on the gates of the town. The panic had indeed been dreadful, but it was now happily over.

Major Wylie again attempted to go to the Place Royale, but he was instantly surrounded by a clamorous multitude, who, knowing him by his dress to be an aide-de-camp of the Duke, angrily exclaimed, "What is the reason that nothing is done for our security? Are we to be left here abandoned to the enemy? Are we to be given up to the French in this way? Why is not the City Guard ordered out to defend the town?" (The City Guard to defend the town from the French!) We could not help laughing at the idea of the excellent defence the City Guard of Brussels would make against the French army. But the frightened and enraged

Belgians could not be pacified, and they beset poor Major Wylie so unmercifully that he was fain to retreat again within the Hôtel de Flandre.

He told us that the battle of yesterday had been severe, and most obstinately contested. The French, whose superiority of force was so great as to surpass all computation, had borne down with dreadful impetuosity upon our little army. "During all his campaigns, and all the bloody battles of the Peninsula," Major Wylie said, "he had never seen so terrible an onset, nor so desperate an engagement. The British, formed into impenetrable squares, received the French cavalry with their bayonets ; drove them back again and again ; stood firm beneath the fire of their tremendous artillery; and, after many hours' hard fighting, completely repulsed the enemy, and remained masters of the field of battle." Our cavalry had come up in the evening, but too late to take any part in the action. A French general and colonel had come over to the British during the battle, crying "Vive le Roi !" Their names I heard, but they have since escaped my memory :* indeed, the names of men who were base enough treacherously to desert the cause even of a rebel and a tyrant in the hour of danger, which they had openly espoused, ought only to be stamped with everlasting infamy. These men must have been doubly traitors, first to Louis XVIII., and then to Napoleon Buonaparte.

The French were commanded by Marshal Ney,† who,

---

* Since writing the above, I have found that the names of these officers were Lieutenant-General Bourmont and Colonel Clouet. [See Appendix, A.]

† Ney, in his own account of this battle, says, "in spite of my exertions, in spite of the intrepidity and devotion of my troops, my utmost exertions could only maintain me in my position till the close of the

with three divisions of infantry, a strong corps of cavalry (under the command of General Kellerman), and a powerful artillery, could make no impression on one division of British infantry, without any cavalry, and with very little artillery. It was but too true that the greatest part of the brave Highlanders, both men and officers, were amongst the killed and wounded. They fought like heroes, and like heroes they fell—an honour to their country : and on many a Highland hill, and through many a Lowland valley, long will the deeds of these brave men be fondly remembered, and their fate deeply deplored! The 28th had particularly distinguished themselves, and gallantly repulsed the French in every attack. Our friend Major Llewellyn was safe ; and I scarcely knew whether the assurance of his safety, or that he and Sir Philip Belson had been in time for the battle, gave me the most heartfelt pleasure. Our loss had been severe, but that of the enemy much greater ; but though our loss was less in actual numbers, it was much more important to us than that which the enemy had sustained was to them. From their great superiority of force, the killed and wounded fell proportionably heavier on our small army, while theirs was scarcely felt among their tremendous hosts.

When Major Wylie came away, about half-past four in the morning, the Duke had made every disposition for battle, in the full expectation that a general engagement would take place this day.* "The Prussians had fought like lions," Major Wylie said; not, however, like British lions, for it was but

day." He then complains grievously of having had *only* three divisions to fight against the British, and boasts of what he *would have done* if he had had five.—*Vide Marshal Ney's Letter.*

* Subsequently, the news of the defeat and retreat of the Prussians obliged the Duke of Wellington also to retreat, to keep open the communications with Blucher.

too true that they had been defeated and repulsed, though we could scarcely at the time give entire credit to this disagreeable news. Waggon-loads of Prussians now began to arrive. Belgic soldiers, covered with dust and blood, and faint with fatigue and pain, came on foot into the town. The moment in which I first saw some of these unfortunate people was, I think, one of the most painful I ever experienced, and soon, very soon, they arrived in numbers. At every jolt of the slow waggons upon the rough pavement we seemed to feel the excruciating pain which they must suffer. Sick to the very heart with horror, I re-entered the hotel, and, in answer to something Major Wylie said to me, I could only exclaim that the wounded were coming in. " Good God! how pale you look! For God's sake do not be alarmed," said the good-natured Major Wylie, compassionately laying his hand upon my arm; "I do assure you there is nothing to fear. The wounded must come here at any rate—it has nothing to do with a defeat." Long familiarised himself to such scenes, they now made no impression upon him, and it never occurred to him to imagine that we could be shocked by seeing anything so common as waggons filled with wounded soldiers. He thought it was the victory or the approach of the French that I feared.

Again, however, he strongly recommended us to set off immediately. If the army should have to retreat, and fall back upon Brussels, which, considering the immense force of the enemy, he said, was not improbable, the confusion in Brussels would be dreadful, and escape impossible. The French might even take the town, and then our situation would be horrible indeed. Of the prudence and wisdom of this advice there could be no doubt. We had experienced the utter impracticability of getting away in the moment of danger ; we knew not how soon that moment might return. Had we ourselves possessed the means of escape, like Mr. and Mrs. H. and others, who had horses of their own, nothing could have induced us to have left Brussels to the last; but to remain exposed to incessant alarm and to imminent danger, in an open town, which before night might be in possession of a merciless enemy, whose formidable armies were threatening it in two separate divisions, at the distance of a very few leagues, seemed certainly little less than madness. With extreme reluctance we at last determined to set out for Antwerp. The Wilsons, though they had carriage-horses, were on the point of setting off; the carriages of Lady F. S. and Lady C. were also at their doors, the trunks and imperiales were tying on with the utmost dispatch, though they had at all times the means of escape within their power.

Our faithless cocher now declared he was willing to go with us, as the French, he said, were not *yet* come—and to Antwerp accordingly we consented to repair. We had had no breakfast all this time, nor would it ever have occurred to us to procure any, had not the sight of Major Wylie's breakfast-tray reminded us of our own famishing state. We swallowed some coffee and bread, sitting on one of the window-seats of the staircase of the Hôtel de Flandre, and then with great regret set off, casting "many a longing, lingering look behind," with feelings of anxiety so deep and overwhelming for the fate and success of our army, that it engrossed all our faculties. Upon the event of the impending battle, which we fully believed this very day was to decide, depended not only the present as well as the future peace and security of Belgium and of Europe ; but, what I confess was to us even yet more dear, the safety and the glory of our gallant army. Absorbed in these reflections, as we slowly made our way out of the town, we witnessed many a melancholy sight ; crowds of afflicted people were assembled round their poor wounded countrymen who had been brought in from the field. One soldier was dying at the door of his own house: the sobs and lamentations of some of the crowd who were collected round him, and the grief marked on their countenances, proclaimed them to be near relations of the unfortunate sufferer. Quite in the suburbs, some poor people were hanging over the insensible corpses of two soldiers who had died of their wounds. The streets were crowded so as to be scarcely passable : carriages were driving past each other as fast as the horses could go. All Brussels seemed to be running away; and the only competition appeared to be who should run the fastest. The road was thronged with people on horseback and on foot flying from the battle, while scattered parties of troops, British, Belgic, Hanoverian, Nassau, and Prussian, were hurrying to the scene of action. A great number of Prussian Lancers, with their black mustachios, high caps, long pikes, and little horses, were pushing forwards to the field. Long trains of commissariat waggons were rolling along with a deafening clatter; overturned carts, and the remains of broken wheels, were lying in the ditches. By the wayside, and beneath the shade of some tall trees, there was a large rude sort of encampment, consisting of men and women, horses and waggons, amongst which universal uproar seemed to prevail. I could have fancied them a Tartar settlement in the act of suddenly decamping at the approach of some horde of savage enemies. Farther on, parks of artillery were drawn up in the peaceful verdant meadows. Droves of oxen were going up to be slaughtered for the army, and the poor beasts, amazed at the horrid objects and noises which they encountered, took fright, and ran about in every direction except the right one, entirely blocking up the road, where confusion reigned unbounded: while the barking of the dogs, the blows and halloos of the drivers, the curses of the soldiers, and the vexation of the passengers, only served to increase the turbulence of the unruly cattle. The canal, by the side of which the road is carried, was covered with boats, and trackschuyts, and côches d'eau, and vessels of every description, and presented a scene of tumult and confusion scarcely inferior to that upon land.

About three miles from Brussels, situated upon an eminence above the road, we passed the magnificent palace of Lacken. I shuddered as I looked up to its lofty dome, and recollected that Napoleon had made the boast that this very night he would sleep beneath its roof. Uncertain, as we then were, how the day that had risen might terminate, believing as we did that the eventful battle was even now begun which was to decide the fate of Europe, my heart swelled with the proud confidence, that unprepared, unconcentrated, outnumbered as they were; leagued with foreigners who could not be depended upon, and with allies who had been defeated, yet that under every disadvantage British valour would still be triumphant, as it had ever been in every contest, and at every period. Great numbers of wounded stragglers from the field were slowly and painfully wandering along the road, pale and faint from loss of blood, and with their heads, arms, and legs bound up with bloody bandages. We spoke to several of them, but they were all either Belgic or Prussian, and did not understand a word of French. Two of the most severely wounded we took upon our carriage and carried into Malines, where they told the côcher their friends lived. From him we learnt that they had been wounded in the battle yesterday morning. I saw— I am sorry to say—one young English gentleman, who was travelling quite alone in his own carriage, sternly order down two of these unfortunate wounded men from his carriage.

The wounded, however, whom we saw, were able to move. In time they would reach a place of safety and shelter; but, if even their sufferings were so great that the very sight of them was painful, what must be the state of those who were left bleeding on the field of the lost battle, deserted by the retreating Prussians, passed by, unpitied and unaided, by the advancing French, and abandoned to perish in sufferings from the bare idea of which humanity recoils!* The day was unusually sultry; but if we felt the rays of the sun beneath which we journeyed to be so oppressive, what must be the situation of the poor unsheltered wounded, exposed to its fervid blaze in the open field, without even a drop of water to cool their thirst? What must be the sufferings of

* Not even imagination could form an idea of the dreadful sufferings that the unfortunate soldiers of the French and Prussian armies, who were wounded in the battles of the 15th and 16th of June, were condemned to endure. It was not until nearly a week afterwards that surgical aid, or assistance of any kind, was given to them. During all this time they remained exposed to the burning heat of the noonday sun, the heavy rains, and the chilling dews of midnight, without any sustenance except what their importunity extorted from the country people, and without any protection even from the flies that tormented them. Numbers had expired; the most trifling wounds had festered, and amputation in almost every instance had become necessary. This, and every other necessary operation, was hastily and negligently performed by the Prussian surgeons. The description I heard of this scene of horror, from some respectable Belgic gentlemen who were spectators of it on the Wednesday following, is too dreadful to repeat.

our own unfortunate men, above all, of those who were not only wounded but prisoners, and at the mercy of the merciless French ? Never—never till this moment, had I any conception of the horrors of war! and they have left an impression on my mind which no time can efface. Dreadful, indeed, is the sight of pain and misery we have no power to relieve, but far more dreadful are the horrors imagination pictures of the scene of carnage; the agonies of the wounded and the dying on the field of battle, where even the dead who had fallen by the sword, in the prime of youth and health, are to be envied!—the thought was agony, and yet I could not banish it from my mind.

At a little inn, half-way to Malines, we got out of the carriage while the horses were eating their rye-bread, and the poor people of the village crowded around us with faces of the greatest consternation and distress, to inquire what had happened. They had heard such varying and contradictory reports that they knew not what to believe, but terror was the predominant feeling ; and their horror of the approach of the French, which they were convinced would happen sooner or later, surpassed everything I could have imagined. In spite of all we could say to inspire confidence, and to convince them that the English had been, and would still be, victorious, and that the French would never again be masters of Belgium, their apprehensions completely overpowered their hopes; and their alarm and consternation were truly pitiable. I asked them why they feared the French so much? With one accord they immediately burst out into exclamations, that they would plunder and destroy everything, and rob and murder them;—that they were monsters, who had no pity, and would show no mercy:—" Oh ! what

will become of us! what will become of us!" was the universal cry of these poor affrighted peasants. They were
anxious about the Duke of Brunswick, and when they heard
that he had really fallen (which we had learnt from Major
Wylie), their lamentations were great, and the certainty of
his fate seemed to increase their despondency. He must
have been a good prince whose fate could at such a moment
be deplored. He had a country seat in the neighbourhood
of Lacken, and he was consequently well known and much
beloved in this part of the country. An officer in a dark
military great coat, whom I took for a German, hearing me
talk to some poor affrighted women with babies in their
arms, whom I was endeavouring to reassure, asked me in
French if I had come from Brussels, and what was the issue
of yesterday's battle? I told him all the particulars I knew,
and after some minutes' conversation, he said at last, with the
air of a person paying a compliment, that he understood *some*
of my countrymen had behaved most gallantly : " comme
braves hommes," was his expression. " Some of my countrymen!" I indignantly exclaimed, feeling myself turn as red
as fire at this foreigner's degrading and partial praise of the
British army—" they all behaved most gallantly, they fought
like heroes; how else should the French have been repulsed:
and when did the English behave otherwise?" " The
English ! but you are not English surely, madame ?" said
the officer. " Oui, monsieur," said I, proudly, " je suis
Anglaise." " Et moi aussi," said he, half laughing ; and
during the short time our conversation lasted, we conde-
scended to make use of our mother-tongue. He proved to
be an English officer going from Antwerp to join the army,
and I took him for a German, chiefly I think because he

accosted me in French, and because he did not look much like an Englishman. Why he took me for a Belgian, heaven only knows: it was not likely that a Belgic lady should be speaking in French to the Belgic people, rather than in the common language of the country.

A party of Nassau troops, on their way to the army, were sitting drinking in some long Flemish waggons at the door of the inn. A Prussian hussar, whom we had passed on the road, arrived while we were there. The moment he dismounted from his horse he was assailed by the Nassau soldiers for news of the battle. While he was telling them his story, anxiety for intelligence made me draw as near as I durst. The loud voices of the soldiers, however, drowned the greater part of his recital, and their language was so barbarous that I could only make out that they were making a joke of Louis XVIII., and laughing at the idea of the fright he would be in, and saying, that he was so fat and unwieldy he would never be able to run away before Napoleon's long legs overtook him. The hussar, seeing me, I suppose, gazing at him very wistfully, respectfully took off his cap, which encouraged me to ask him if I had not misunderstood him, that I thought I had heard him say the French had beaten the Prussians. "No, madame," said he, with an air of great concern, "it is really so; the French have beaten the Prussians." "The French beat the Prussians!" I exclaimed: "Did you say, sir, that the French had beaten the Prussians? are you sure of it?" "Too sure, madame, for I was in the battle." I now perceived for the first time that he was slightly wounded; his long blue cloak, which nearly descended to his feet, had concealed it. He told us that, after a desperate engagement, the Prussians had been

repulsed and compelled to retreat, and that the French were
advancing in great force. We had repeatedly heard this at
Brussels; but, unwilling to believe bad news, we had hoped
it would prove false, and even yet we would gladly have
taken refuge in incredulity.

The garçon of this inn, a fine youth, with a most engaging
countenance, was in great anxiety and alarm at the approach
of the French, and he implored us to tell him the whole
truth; for if they should come, it would cost him his life,
and he would fly to the end of the world to avoid them. We
assured him that the French had been repulsed yesterday by
the British, when our force was not half collected, and that,
now that the cavalry and all the troops had joined the army,
there could be no doubt that the English would be victorious. "Ah! je l'espère!" said the garçon; "mais ils sont
terribles, ces François." We assured him that terrible as
they were, they would never conquer the British and Belgic
army, nor regain possession of Belgium. The garçon fer-
vently prayed they never might:—"Mais, je ne sais quoi
faire, moi," said this poor youth in his Belgic French, with
a face of extreme perplexity, as we drove off.

Of the town of Malines I do not retain the smallest
remembrance; but the consternation of the people with
whom it was crowded, and their faces of terror and distress,
I shall never forget. They were struck with universal
dismay, and so thoroughly convinced that Napoleon would
be victorious, that we might as well have talked to the winds
as have told them that he would be defeated. They only
shook their heads, and despondingly said: "Ah! he has so
many soldiers, and he is so desperate—and he cares not how
many thousands he sacrifices; he cares for nothing but his

ambition:—Oh! he will be here, that is too certain." The
garçon of this inn had been a conscript, and served two years
in the French army. At the expiration of that period he
had procured a substitute for one thousand florins, which
money, I suspect, he had amassed by plunder. He was, however, a most intelligent man, and his hatred of the French,
and of Napoleon in particular, was so strong, that he could
not refrain from pouring out a most eloquent torrent of invective against him: "And throughout the whole of Belgium
he is equally dreaded and detested in every place—except at
Antwerp," added he, correcting himself; "there he has some
adherents, for many people grew rich by the public works,
and by making the docks, and building the ships, and sup-
plying the arsenal; and many grew rich upon the distresses
of the people—and therefore they wish for him back again."
My brother observed that he had certainly done a great deal
for Antwerp, and made great improvements, and he particularly mentioned the docks and the quays.

"Yes! he did a great many fine things, to be sure, at
Antwerp, and he took care to make us pay for them. Au
reste," continued he, "the people of Antwerp, that is, the
merchants and the manufacturers, and all the decent, industrious people, hate him with their whole hearts." "And
why do the Belgians hate him so much?" I asked. "Why!
because he stopped our trade; he ruined our manufactures
and commerce; he took our men to fight his battles, and our
money to fill his pockets; and he took from us the means to
get money: here, in this very town, the lace manufacturers
were starved; the work-women had no employment; our
streets were filled with beggars; our priests were insulted:
he destroyed, he consumed everything." "Il a mangé tout,"

was the phrase he frequently repeated, with an expression of
hatred in his voice and gesture so strong that I can give no
idea of it. "But he cannot live without war, nor can the
French; it is their trade; they live by it; they make their
fortunes by it; they place all their 'hopes in it; they are
wolves that prey upon other nations; they live by blood and
plunder: they are true banditti (vrais brigands), and they
are so cruel, so wicked—ils sont si méchans." It is impossible
to give the force of this expression in a literal translation.
When we asked him if the Belgians did not dislike the
Dutch, and if the government of the House of Orange was
not unpopular, he said, "Je vous dirai, monsieur: Les Hol-
landais et les Belges never liked each other, and one great
reason is the difference of our religion.   They think us
Papists and bigots, and we think them Puritans and Cal-
vinists; besides, we were always rivals, and always jealous of
each other, and we think (c'est à dire les Belges) that their
king becoming our king, is, as if we had fallen under their
dominion.   If we may not be an independent nation, we
would, perhaps, rather belong to the English, or to the
Austrians; but we would rather belong to anything—to the
devil himself—than to Napoleon Buonaparte."

The poor lace-makers whom we saw were in nervous
trepidation at the expected approach of the dreaded French,
whom they reviled with all the bitterness and volubility of
female eloquence.   The same sentiments were written upon
every countenance, and uttered by every tongue.   In every
village and every hamlet through which we passed, the
utmost consternation seemed to reign.   We met officers on
horseback, and detachments of troops marching to join the
army.   It was with difficulty I refrained from beseeching

them to hasten forwards: it seemed to me that every man was of importance. At another time I might have been interested with seeing the country; but now—I could not look at it—I could not think of it; and as my eye rested with a vacant gaze upon the waving fields of luxuriant corn through which we passed, I could only feel the heart-sickening dread, that the harvests of Belgium, though they had been sown in peace, would be reaped in blood. We had every reason to think that the mortal struggle had been renewed; Lord Wellington himself, the whole army expected it. How then was it possible, believing, as we did, that, within a few leagues of us, the battle was at that time raging that was to decide the fate of Europe, and give or take from our gallant countrymen the palm of victory and of glory—that we could for a single instant feel the smallest interest about anything else?

At a distance, we saw the lofty spire of the cathedral of Antwerp, without *then* admiring its beauty, or even being conscious that it was beautiful. We looked, we felt, indeed, like moving automatons. Our persons were there, but our minds were absent. Every step we took only seemed to increase our solicitude for all we left behind. Our thoughts still to the battle

> "turned with ceaseless pain,
> And dragged at each remove a lengthening chain."

A tremendous storm of thunder and lightning and rain burst over our heads. It was peculiarly awful. But what are the thunder and lightnings of heaven to the thunder and lightnings of war, which, perhaps, at this very moment, were sweeping away thousands! The thunderbolts of

God are merciful and harmless; those of men deadly and destructive. We thought of this storm, as of everything else, only with reference to our army—to those who were fighting, and those who were bleeding on the field of battle, and who were exposed unsheltered to its rage.

We gazed with admiration at the threatening walls and ancient battlements of Antwerp, which are encircled with a wooden palisade. This seemed a complete work of supererogation, and struck me as being something like putting a strong box of iron into a band-box of pasteboard for further security.* Three walls of immense strength and thickness, surrounded by three broad deep ditches or moats, lay one behind another. To an ignorant, unpractised eye like mine, its fortifications seemed to be impregnable; and as we passed under its gloomy gates, and slowly crossed its sounding draw-bridges, I heartily wished that the whole British army were safe within its walls.—This was certainly more " a woman's than a warrior's wish." Antwerp was already crowded with fugitives from Brussels; and with considerable difficulty we got the accommodation of two very small rooms in the hotel of Le Grand Laboureur, in the Place de Maire.

No later authentic intelligence than that which we had heard previously to leaving Brussels had been received here; reports of all kinds assailed us, as quick and varying as the tints of the evening clouds, but we could learn nothing; the commandant knew nothing; we could not even ascertain whether another engagement had taken place

---

* This was, I find, only a proof of my ignorance; I afterwards learnt that wooden palisades add greatly to the strength of fortifications.

to-day, and in miserable suspense we passed the remainder of the evening.

One of the apartments in our hotel was occupied by the corpse of the Duke of Brunswick, which had arrived about two o'clock. It had been already embalmed, and was now placed in its first coffin. My brother went to see it: but the room was so crowded with guards and soldiers, British and foreign military, and with people of every description, that neither my sister nor I chose to go. My brother described the countenance as remarkably placid and noble; serene even in death. It was past midnight: my brother and sister had gone to rest, and I was sitting alone, listening to the incessant torrents of rain which drove furiously against the windows, and thinking of our army, who were lying on the cold, wet ground, overcome with toil, and exposed to all "the pelting of the pitiless storm." Everything was silent, —when I heard, all at once, the dismal sounds of nailing down the coffin of the Duke of Brunswick. It was a solemn and affecting sound; it was the last knell of the departed princely warrior: when at length it ceased, and all again was silent, I went down with the young woman of the house, to look at the last narrow mansion of this brave and unfortunate prince. Tapers were burning at the head and foot of the coffin. The room was now cleared of all, excepting two Brunswick officers who were watching over it, and whose pale, mournful countenances, sable uniforms, and black nodding plumes, well accorded with this gloomy chamber of death. It was but yesterday that this prince, in the flower of life and fortune, went out to the field full of military ardour, and gloriously fell in battle, leading on his soldiers to the charge. He was the first of the noble warriors who fell on the memorable field of Quatre Bras. But he has lived long enough who has lived to acquire glory: he dies a noble death who dies for his country. The Duke of Brunswick lived and died like a hero, and he has left his monument in the hearts of his people, by whom his fate will be long and deeply lamented; and by future times his memory will be honoured.

It seemed to be my invariable lot at the dead hour of the night to be disturbed with some new and terrible alarm. I had not returned many minutes to my room, after this visit to the remains of departed greatness, and I was just preparing to go to bed, when I suddenly heard the well-known hateful sounds of the rolling of heavy military carriages, passing rapidly through the streets, which were instantly succeeded by the trampling of horses' feet, the clamour of voices, and all the hurry of alarm. The streets seemed thronged with people. Concluding that some news must have arrived, I hastily went out to the little apartment which the young woman of the house occupied, and where she told me at any hour she was to be found—but she was gone, and the noise below was so great, and the men's voices so loud, that I durst not venture down stairs. I wandered along the passages, and hung over the balustrades of the staircase, listening to this increasing noise in a state of the most painful suspense. At last the girl returned with a countenance of consternation, and pale as death. I eagerly inquired if there was any news. She said that there was; the very worst;—that all was lost; that our army had been compelled to retreat, and were falling back upon Brussels: the French pursuing them. All the English had left Brussels. People in carriages, on horseback, and on foot, were flying into

Antwerp in the greatest dismay. Baggage waggons, ammunition, and artillery, were pouring into the town on all sides: and " enfin, madame," said she, " tout est perdu!"

For a few minutes, consternation overpowered all my faculties. The English retreating, pursued by the French, overwhelmed by a tremendous superiority of numbers—our gallant countrymen vainly sacrificed—the flower of our army laid low—Buonaparte and the French triumphant!—the thought was not to be borne: till this moment I never knew the bitterness, the intensity of my detestation of them. It never occurred to me to doubt that there had been a battle, and it seemed too probable that its result had been unfavourable to the British. I hoped, however, that they were only retreating in consequence of their extreme inferiority of force to the enemy, to wait until they were joined either by the fresh reinforcements of our own troops which were expected, or by the Russians. Some experienced officers had thought this might probably happen, even when the troops first marched out of Brussels. I recollected Lord Wellington entrenching himself in the lines of Torres Vedras. I recalled with proud confidence the multiplied triumphs of my countrymen in arms, and I firmly believed that, whatever might be the temporary reverses, or appearance of reverse, they would eventually prove victorious.

But in vain I endeavoured to reassure this poor terrified girl, or inspire her with the conviction I felt myself, that though the English might retreat before an overpowering force, against which it would be madness to keep the field, they only retreated to advance with more strength; and that when joined by fresh reinforcements they would give battle, and beat the French; and that with such a general

and such an army, they never had been, and they never could
be, defeated.

I succeeded much better in inspiring myself with hope and
confidence than this poor young woman; but all that I myself endured during this long night of misery is not to be
imagined or described. The uncertain fate of our army,
their critical situation, and the dread that some serious
reverse had befallen them, filled my mind with the most
dreadful apprehensions. Worn out as I had been with two
successive nights of sleepless alarm, this news had effectually
murdered sleep; and even when fatigue for a few minutes
overpowered my senses, I started up again with a sense of
horror to listen to the beating of the heavy torrents of rain,
and the dismal sounds of alarm which filled the streets; the
rattle of carriages continually driving to the door, crowded
with fugitives who vainly solicited to be taken in, and drove
away utterly at a loss where to find a place of shelter; and
the deafening noise of the rolling of heavy military waggons
which, during the whole night, never ceased a single moment.
So deep was the impression these sounds made upon my
senses, so associated had they now become with feelings of
dismay and alarm, that long after every terror was ended
in the glorious certainty of victory, I never could hear the
rattling of these carriages, and the thundering of their
wheels, without a sensation of horror that went to my very
heart.

The morning—the eventful morning of Sunday, the 18th
of June—rose, darkened by clouds and mists, and driving rain.
Amongst the rest of the fugitives, our friends, the Hon. Mr.
and Mrs. H., arrived about seven o'clock, and, after considerable
difficulty and delay, succeeded in obtaining a wretched little

hole in a private house, with a miserable pallet bed, and destitute of all other furniture; but they were too glad to find shelter, and too thankful to get into a place of safety, to complain of these inconveniences; and overcome with fatigue, they went immediately to bed. It was not without considerable difficulty and danger that their carriage had got out of the choked-up streets of Brussels, and made its way to Malines, where they had been, for a time, refused shelter. At length, the golden arguments Mr. H. used obtained for them admittance into a room filled with people of all sexes, ages, countries, and ranks—French Princes and foreign Counts, and English Barons, and Right Honourable ladies and gentlemen, together with a considerable mixture of less dignified beings, were all lying together, outstretched upon the tables, the chairs, and the floor; some groaning, and some complaining, and many snoring, and almost all of them completely drenched with rain. The water streamed from Mr. H.'s clothes, who had driven his own carriage. In this situation, they, too, lay down and slept, while their horses rested; and then, at break of day, pursued their flight. A hundred Napoleons had been vainly offered for a pair of horses but a few hours after we left Brussels, and the scene of panic and confusion which it presented on Saturday evening surpassed all conception. The certainty of the defeat of the Prussians; of their retreat; and of the retreat of the British army, prepared the people to expect the worst. Aggravated reports of disaster and dismay continually succeeded to each other: the despair and lamentations of the Belgians, the anxiety of the English to learn the fate of their friends who had been in the battle the preceding day; the dreadful spectacle of the waggon loads of wounded coming in, and the terrified fugitives flying out in momentary expectation of the arrival of the French:—the streets, the roads, the canals covered with boats, carriages, waggons, horses, and crowds of unfortunate people, flying from this scene of horror and danger, formed altogether a combination of tumult, terror, and misery which cannot be described. Numbers, even of ladies, unable to procure any means of conveyance, set off on foot, and walked in the dark, beneath the pelting storm, to Malines; and the distress of the crowds who now filled Antwerp, it is utterly impossible to conceive. We were, however, soon inexpressibly relieved, by hearing that there had been no engagement of any consequence the preceding day; that the British army had fallen back seven miles in order to take up a position more favourable for the cavalry, and for communication with the Prussians; that they were now about nine miles from Brussels; and that a general and, most probably, decisive action would inevitably take place to-day.

Although it continued to rain, we set out, for to sit still in the house was impossible, and after passing through several streets, we went into the cathedral, where high mass was performing, and

> "Where through the long-drawn aisle and fretted vault
> The pealing anthem swell'd the note of praise."

For a while its solemn harmony seemed to calm the fever of my mind; it elevated my thoughts to that God, in whose unerring wisdom and divine mercy I could alone at this awful moment put my trust, and to Him "who is the only giver of victory," and at whose command empires rise and fall, flourish and decay; to Him who alone has power to save and to destroy, I breathed a silent prayer to bless the British arms, to shield my brave and heroic countrymen in

the hour of danger, and give to them the success and glory
of the battle. Intelligence arrived that the action had commenced. We were told that the French had attacked the
British this morning at daybreak: the contending armies
were actually engaged, and the last, the dreadful battle was
at this very moment deciding.

It is impossible for any but those who have actually experienced it to conceive the dreadful, the overwhelming anxiety
of being so near such eventful scenes, without being actually
engaged in them; to know that within a few leagues the
dreadful storm of war is raging in all its horrors, and the
mortal conflict going forward which is to decide the glory
of your country, and the security of the world:—to think
that while you are sitting in passive inactivity, or engaged
in the most trifling occupations, your brave countrymen are
fighting and falling in the uncertain battle, and your friends,
and those whose fate you may deplore through life, perhaps
at that very moment breathing their last; to be surrounded
by misery that you cannot console, and sufferings that you
cannot relieve; to wait, to look, to long in vain for intelligence; to be distracted with a thousand confused and contradictory accounts without being able to ascertain the truth;
to be at one moment elevated with hope, and the next de-
pressed with fear; to endure the long-protracted suspense—
the deep-wrought feelings of expectation—the incessant
alarms, the ever-varying reports—the dreadful rumours of
evil—Oh! it was a state of misery almost too great, too
agonising for human endurance! Never—never shall I
forget the torturing suspense, the intense anxiety of mind,
and agitation of spirit, in which this day was passed. In
the midst of all that could interest the mind and charm the

F

fancy, and surrounded by all that, at any other time, would have afforded me the highest gratification, I could neither see, hear, observe, admire, nor understand anything; I could think of nothing but the battle. In vain I tried to distract my thoughts, or to force my attention even for a moment to other things: the situation of our army, their danger, their success, their sufferings, and their glory, were for ever present to me. Unable to rest, we wandered mechanically about the town, regardless of the frequent heavy showers of rain, and of the deep and dirty streets, anxiously awaiting the arrival of news from the army—though well aware that for many hours nothing could be known of the event of the battle. With a view to dissipate our fruitless anxiety, and as a shelter from the rain, we visited several cabinets of paintings: but I beheld the noblest works of art, and the finest monuments of departed genius, with indifference. Not even the sublime touches, the affecting images, and the unrivalled productions of Guido, and Raphael, and Rubens; not all the force, the pathos, and the expression of their powerful genius, could at this moment charm or even interest me; for I had no power to feel their beauties.

Every faculty of our minds was absorbed in one feeling, one thought, one interest;—we seemed like bodies without souls. Our persons and our outward senses were indeed present in Antwerp, but our whole hearts and souls were with the army.

In the course of our wanderings we met many people whom we knew, and had much conversation with many whom we did not know. At this momentous crisis, one feeling actuated every heart—one thought engaged every tongue—one common interest bound together every human being. All ranks were confounded; all distinctions levelled; all common forms neglected. Gentlemen and servants; lords and common soldiers; British and foreigners, were all upon an equality—elbowing each other without ceremony, and addressing each other without apology. Ladies accosted men they had never before seen with eager questions without hesitation; strangers conversed together like friends, and English reserve seemed no longer to exist. From morning till night the great Place de Maire was completely filled with people, standing under umbrellas, and eagerly watching for news of the battle; so closely packed was this anxious crowd, that, when viewed from the hotel windows, nothing could be seen but one compact mass of umbrellas. As the day advanced, the consternation became greater. The number of terrified fugitives from Brussels, upon whose faces were marked the deepest anxiety and distress, and who thronged into the town on horseback and on foot, increased the general dismay, while long rows of carriages lined the streets, filled with people who could find no place of shelter.

Troops from the Hanseatic towns marched in to strengthen the garrison of the city in case of a siege. Long trains of artillery, ammunition, military stores, and supplies of all sorts incessantly poured in, and there seemed to be no end of the heavy waggons that rolled through the streets. Reports more and more gloomy reached our ears; every hour only served to add to the general despondency. On every side we heard that the battle was fought under circumstances so disadvantageous to the British, and against a preponderance of force so overpowering, that it was impossible it could be won. Long did we resist the depressing impression these alarming accounts were calculated to make upon our minds;

long did we believe, in spite of every unfavourable appearance, that the British would be victorious. Towards evening a wounded officer arrived, bringing intelligence that the onset had been most terrible, and so immense were the numbers of the enemy, that he "did not believe it was in the power of man to save the battle." To record the innumerable false reports we heard spread by the terrified fugitives, who continually poured into the town from Brussels, would be endless. At length, after an interval of the most torturing suspense, a wounded British officer of hussars, scarcely able to sit his horse, and faint from loss of blood, rode up to the door of the hotel, and told us the disastrous tidings, that the battle was lost, and that Brussels, by this time, was in the possession of the enemy. He said, that in all the battles he had ever been engaged in, he had never witnessed anything at all equal to the horrors of this. The French had fought with the most desperate valour, but, when he left the field, they had been repulsed by the British at every point with immense slaughter: the news of the defeat had, however, overtaken him on the road; all the baggage belonging to the army was taken or destroyed, and the confusion among the French at Vittoria, he said, was nothing to this. He had himself been passed by panic-struck fugitives from the field, flying for their lives, and he had been obliged to hurry forward, notwithstanding his wounds, in order to effect his escape. Two gentlemen from Brussels corroborated this dreadful account: in an agitation that almost deprived them of the power of utterance, they declared that when they came away, Brussels presented the most dreadful scene of tumult, horror, and confusion; that intelligence had been received of the complete defeat of the

British, and that the French were every moment expected. The carnage had been most tremendous. The Duke of Wellington, they said, was severely wounded; Sir Dennis Pack killed; and all our bravest officers killed, wounded, or prisoners. In vain we inquired, where, if the battle was lost, where was now, and what had become of the British army? —" God alone knows," was the answer. The next moment we heard from a gentleman who had just arrived, that before he left Brussels, the French had actually entered it; that he had himself seen a party of them; and another gentleman (apparently an officer) declared he had been pursued by them more than half way to Malines!

Dreadful was the panic and dismay that now seized the unfortunate Belgians, and in the most piercing tones of horror and despair they cried out, that the French would be at the gates before morning. Some English people, thinking Antwerp no longer safe, set off for Breda, late as it was. Later still, accounts were brought (as we were told) by three British officers, confirming the dreadful tidings of defeat; it was even said that the French were already at Malines. We believed, we trusted that these reports of evil were greatly exaggerated; we did not credit their dreadful extent, but that some terrible reverse had befallen the British army it was no longer possible to doubt. During the whole of this dreadful night, the consternation, the alarm, the tumult, the combination of horrid noises that filled the streets, I shall never forget. The rapid rolling of the carriages, the rattle of artillery, and the slow, heavy motion of the large waggons filled with wounded soldiers, which incessantly entered the town, were the most dismal of all.

Of the bitter agony, the deep-seated affliction that now

overwhelmed us, it would be in vain to speak. There are
feelings in the human heart that can find no utterance in
words, and which " lie too deep for tears :" and the conviction
that the British army had been defeated—the dreadful uncertainty of its fate—and the heart-piercing sight of my brave,
my unfortunate wounded countrymen returning from the
lost battle in which their valour had been exerted, and their
blood been shed in vain, awakened sensations which no
visible emotion, no power of language could express; but
which have left an impression on my mind that no lapse of
time can efface. No private calamity, however great, that
had befallen myself individually, could have afflicted me
with such bitter anguish as I now suffered. The image of
the British troops retreating before a conquering, an insulting,
a merciless enemy—defeated, perhaps cut to pieces : the idea
of their misfortunes and their sufferings—of the wounded
abandoned to perish on the fatal field ; the misery of thousands; the distress in which it would plunge my country;
the years of war and bloodshed, and all the dreadful consequences it would bring upon the world, incessantly haunted
my mind during this long night of misery. Overpowered
by three days and nights of extreme fatigue, anxiety, and
agitation, I fell at times into a sort of unquiet slumber; but
my busy fancy still presented the horrid images of terror and
distress, and repeatedly I started up from uneasy sleep to the
dreadful consciousness of waking misery. Oh ! it was a night
of unspeakable horror—

> " Nor when morning came
> Did the realities of light and day
> Bring aught of comfort: wheresoe'er we went
> The tidings of defeat had gone before;
> And leaving their defenceless homes, to seek
> What shelter walls and battlements might yield,

Old men with feeble feet, and tottering babes,
And widows with their infants in their arms
Hurried along: nor royal festival,
Nor sacred pageant—with like multitude
E'er fill'd the public way:—all whom the sword
Had spared—fled here!"—*Southey's Roderick.*

With a heavy heart, I rose and dressed myself, and went out before eight o'clock, attended only by our old valet de place, who with a sorrowful countenance awaited me at the foot of the stairs. From him, and from the master of the hotel, who were both on the watch for news, I learned that no official intelligence had been received, no courier had arrived: but no doubt was entertained of the truth of the dreadful reports of the night, and the events of every hour seemed to give full confirmation of the worst. I traversed the gloomy streets, anxiously gazing at every melancholy careworn countenance I met, as if there I could read the truth. I was struck to the heart with horror by the sight of the heavy loaded waggons of wounded soldiers which incessantly passed by me; while litters borne silently along on men's shoulders gave dreadful indications of sufferings more severe, or nearer their final termination; nor were they less painful to the thoughts from being unseen. Imagination perhaps conjured up sufferings more dreadful than the reality —sufferings at which my blood ran cold.

Wholly forgetful of some business I had to transact, which I had undertaken for a friend before leaving England, I hurried through the streets with the vague hope of hearing some decisive intelligence; certain that anything, even the knowledge of the worst, would be preferable to this state of wretchedness and torturing suspense. At last, without intending it, I found myself near the Malines gate. Conducted by the old valet, I turned into a narrow street on my right, where, to my inexpressible astonishment, I saw five wounded Highland soldiers who, in spite of the bandages which enveloped their heads, arms, and legs, were shouting and huzzaing with the vociferous demonstrations of joy. In answer to my eager questions, they told me that a courier had that moment entered the town from the Duke of Wellington, bringing an account that the English had gained a complete victory, that the remains of the French army were in full retreat, and the English in pursuit of them.

To the last hour of my life, never shall I forget the sensations of that moment. Scarcely daring to credit the extent of this wonderful, this transporting news, I did, however, believe that the English had gained the victory; believed it with feelings to which no language can do justice, and which found relief in tears of joy that I could not repress. For some minutes I was unable to speak. The overpowering emotions which filled my heart were far too powerful for expression; but the boon of life to the wretch whose head is laid upon the block could scarcely be received with more transport and gratitude. The sudden transition from the depth of despair to joy unutterable, was almost too great to be borne.

In the mean time the Highlanders, regardless of their wounds, their fatigues, their dangers, and their sufferings, kept throwing up their Highland bonnets into the air, and continually vociferating, — " Boney's beat! Boney's beat! hurrah! hurrah! Boney's beat!" Their tumultuous joy attracted round them a number of old Flemish women, who were extremely curious to know the cause of this uproar, and kept gabbling to the soldiers in their own tongue. One of them, more eager than the rest, seized one of the men by his coat, pulling at it, and making the most ludicrous gestures imaginable to induce him to attend to her; while the Highlander, quite forgetting in his transport that the old woman did not understand Scotch, kept vociferating that "Boney was beat, and rinning away till his ain country as fast as he could gang." At any other time, the old Flemish woman, holding the soldier fast, shrugging up her shoulders, and making these absurd grimaces, and the Highlander roaring to her in broad Scotch would have presented a most laughable scene—" Hout, ye auld gowk," cried the good-humoured soldier, " dinna ye ken that Boney's beat— what, are ye deef?—dare say the wife—I say Boney's beat, woman !" When the news was explained to the old women they were in an ecstasy almost as great as that of the Highlanders themselves, and the joy of the old valet was quite unbounded. These poor men were on their way to the hospital, but they did not know which way to go ; they were ignorant of the language, and could not inquire. I thought of sending the valet de place with them, who was extremely willing to conduct " ces bons Ecossois," as he called them, but then I could not easily have found my own way home; so the valet de place, the soldiers, and I, all went to the hospital together. Our progress was slow, for one of them was very lame, another had lost three of the fingers of his right hand, and had a ball lodged in his shoulder. Some of them were from the Highlands, and some from the Lowlands, and when they found that I came from Scotland, and lived upon the Tweed, they were quite delighted. One of them was from the Tweed as well as myself, he said, " he cam' oot o' Peeblesshire."

After parting with them close to the hospital, I returned

homewards, and by the time I reached the Place de Maire it was thronged with multitudes of people, who seemed at a loss how to give vent to their transport. One loud universal buzz of voices filled the streets; one feeling pervaded every heart; one expression beamed on every face: in short, the people were quite wild with joy, and some of them really seemed by no means in possession of their senses. At the door of our hotel the first sight I beheld among the crowds that encircled it, was an English lady, who had apparently attained the full meridian of life, with a night-cap stuck on the top of her head, discovering her hair in papillotes beneath, attired in a long white flannel dressing-gown, loosely tied about her waist, with the sleeves tucked up above the elbows. She was flying about in a distracted manner, with a paper in her hand, loudly proclaiming the glorious tidings, continually repeating the same thing, and rejoicing, lamenting, wondering, pitying, and exclaiming, all in the same breath. From an English gentleman whom I had met, I had already learned all the particulars that were known; but this lady seized upon me, repeated them all again and again, interrupting herself with mourning over the misfortunes of poor Lady de Lancey, pitying Lady F. Somerset, rejoicing in the victory, wondering at the Duke's escape, lamenting for Sir Thomas Picton, and declaring, which was incontestably true, that she herself was quite distracted.

In vain did her maid pursue her about with a great shawl, which occasionally she succeeded in putting upon her shoulders, but which invariably fell off again the next moment.

In vain did another lady, whose dress and mind were rather more composed, endeavour to entice her away—she could not be brought to pay them the smallest attention, and

I left her still talking as fast as ever, and standing in this curious déshabille among gentlemen and footmen, and officers and soldiers, and valets de place, and in full view of the multitudes who thronged the great Place de Maire. An express had arrived, soon after eight o'clock, bringing the Duke of Wellington's bulletin, dated Waterloo, containing a brief account of the glorious battle. But from private letters and accounts we learnt that the triumph of the British arms had indeed been complete. After a most dreadful and sanguinary battle, which lasted from ten in the morning till nine at night, the French at length gave way, and fled in confusion from the field, leaving behind them their artillery, their baggage, their wounded, and their prisoners. The certainty of this great, this glorious victory, won by the heroic valour of our countrymen in circumstances so disadvantageous; the fall of the enemy of Britain and of mankind; the deliverance of Europe; the peace of the world, and, above all, the glory of England, rushed into my mind; and every individual interest, every personal consideration, every other thought and feeling, were swallowed up and forgotten.

The contest had been dreadful—the carnage unexampled in the bloodiest annals of history. The French army had been nearly annihilated, and our loss was tremendous. The greatest part of our gallant army, the best, the bravest of our officers, were among the killed and wounded. Sir Colin Halket, Generals Cooke and Alten, Sir Dennis Pack, the Prince of Orange, Lord Uxbridge,* and Lord Fitzroy Somerset, were severely wounded. Sir Thomas Picton, Sir William Ponsonby, Sir Alexander Gordon were killed. Sir

* Afterwards Marquis of Anglesey

William de Lancey had also been killed by a cannon-ball
while in absolute contact with the Duke, whose escapes
seemed to have been almost miraculous.   Unmindful, perhaps even unconscious, of the showers of shot and shell, he
had stood undaunted from morning till night in the thickest
of the battle, coolly reconnoitring with his glass the motions
of the enemy, issuing his orders with the utmost precision,
and everywhere present by his promptitude, coolness, and
presence of mind.   Almost all his staff officers were either
killed or wounded.*   Lady M. showed us the official bulletin;
it contained a most brief and modest account of the victory,
announcing scarcely any particulars, and mentioning the
names only of a very few of the principal officers who were
among the sufferers.

In a few hours the town was crowded with the wounded.
The regular hospitals were soon filled, and barracks, churches,
and convents were converted into temporary hospitals with
all possible expedition.   Tents were pitched in a large piece
of open ground near the citadel, and numbers of these unfortunate sufferers were carried there : but nothing could
contain the multitude of wounded who continually entered
the town.   Numbers were lying on the hard pavement of
the streets, and on the steps of the houses; and numbers
were wandering about in search of a place of shelter.   Nothing affected me more than the quiet fortitude and uncom-
plaining patience with which these poor men bore their
sufferings.   Not a word, not a murmur, not a groan escaped

---

* At one time, as we afterwards learned, the Duke had scarcely a single
aide-de-camp left to dispatch with orders. All around him fell dead, or
wounded. His preservation was miraculous. As he himself reverentially
declared after the battle, "The finger of God was upon me."

their lips. They lay extended on their backs in the long waggons, their clothes stained with blood, blinded by the intolerable rays of the sun, in silent suffering; while every jolt of the waggons seemed to go to one's very heart. Numbers on foot, almost sinking with fatigue and loss of blood, were slowly and painfully making their way along the streets. Officers supported on their horses, and almost insensible, with faces pale as death, and marked with agony, and those dreadful litters, whose very appearance bespoke torture and death, were passing through every street.

Never shall I forget the impression that the sight of my poor wounded countrymen made upon my mind. When I saw their sufferings, and thought of their deeds in arms, of their dauntless intrepidity in the field, and of the immortal glory they had won, tears of pity, admiration, and gratitude burst from my heart, and I looked at the meanest soldier returning, covered with wounds, from fighting the battles of his country, with a respect and admiration which not all the kings and princes of the earth could have extorted from me.

If such were the horrors of the scene here, what must they be on the field of battle, covered with thousands of the dead, the wounded, and the dying! The idea was almost too dreadful for human endurance; and yet there were those of my own country, and even of my own sex, whom I heard express a longing wish to visit this very morning the fatal field of Waterloo! If, by visiting that dreadful scene of glory and of death, I could have saved the life, or assuaged the pangs, of one individual who had fallen for his country, gladly would I have braved its horrors; but for the gratification of an idle, a barbarous curiosity, to gaze upon the mangled corpses of thousands; to hear the deep groans of agony, and witness the last struggles of the departing spirit —No! worlds should not have bribed me to have encountered the sight: the consolation of being useful, alone could have armed one with courage to have witnessed it. Nothing could exceed the humanity and kindness of the Belgic people to those poor sufferers who now crowded the streets. Unsolicited they took them into their own houses; sent bedding to the hospitals; resigned their own rooms to their use; provided them with every comfort, and administered to their wants as if they had been their own sons. One old lady alone, who was the sole inhabitant of a large house, refused to take in two wounded officers; the Commandant, on hearing of this, immediately billetted six private soldiers upon her. But, notwithstanding the praiseworthy activity and exertion which were used to accommodate them, it was long, long indeed, before they could all be taken care of. We grieved that we had no house to shelter them, and no power to give them any essential relief. Money was to them as useless as the lump of gold to Robinson Crusoe in his desert island: we could not act by them the part of the good Samaritan, nor could we, like the heroines of the days of chivalry, bind up and dress their wounds, for in our ignorance we should only have injured them, and the most stupid hospital mate could perform that office a thousand times better than the finest lady.

Numbers of poor wounded Highlanders were patiently sitting in the streets, shaded from the powerful rays of the sun. We had a good deal of conversation with several of the privates of the 42nd and 92nd regiments, and their account of the battle was most simple and interesting. They seemed not to have the smallest pride in what they had done; but

to consider it quite as a matter of course; they uttered not
the smallest complaint, but rather made light of their sufferings, and there was nothing in their words or manner that
looked as if they were sensible of having done anything in
the least extraordinary; nothing that laid claim to pity,
admiration, or glory. The carnage among the French, both
on the 16th and 18th, in their encounter with the Highland
regiments, was described to us as most dreadful. The cuirassiers, men and officers, horses and riders, were rolled in
death, one upon another, after the British charge with the
bayonet. In vain the French returned to the attack with
furious valour and reinforced numbers. Their utmost efforts
could make no impression on the impenetrable squares of the
infantry, and the spiked wall of the British embattled
bayonets; and when they retired from the ineffectual attack,
the brave Highlanders, with loud cries of "Scotland for ever!"
rushed among them, bore down all resistance, and scattered
their legions like withered leaves before the blast of autumn.

It is but justice to these gallant men to say, that it was
not from themselves we heard this relation of their own
deeds. *They* could not be induced to speak of what they
had done, but it was repeated on every side; it was the
theme of every tongue. The love and admiration of the
whole Belgic people for the Highlanders are most remarkable. Whenever they heard them mentioned, they exclaimed, " Ah! ces braves hommes! ces bons Ecossais! ils
sont si doux—et si aimables—et dans la guerre!—ah! mon
Dieu! comme ils sont terribles!" They never speak of
them without some epithet of affection or admiration. Their
merits are the darling topic of their private circles, and their
figures the favourite signs of their public-houses; in short,

they are the best of soldiers and of men, according to the Belgians—nothing was ever like them, and the idea they have of their valour is quite prodigious.*

The sufferings of the wounded, however, did not form the only affecting sight that Antwerp presented. The deep, the distracting grief of the unfortunate people whose friends had perished, and the heart-rending anxiety of those who vainly sought for intelligence of the fate of those most dear to them, were amongst the most distressing parts of the many mournful scenes we witnessed. Of those friends for whose safety we were deeply solicitous, we could gain no information, and the suspense, dreadful as it was, we, as well as thousands, were obliged to endure. But our anxiety, our sorrows, seemed light indeed in comparison with those of others: there were few who had not some near friend or relative to deplore, and Antwerp was filled with heart-broken mourners, whom the victory of yesterday had bereft of all that made life dear to them. In the same hotel with us was poor Lady de Lancey, a young and widowed bride, upon whom, in all the hopes of happiness—in the very flower of youth—unacquainted with sorrow, and far from every friend, the heaviest stroke of affliction had fallen unprepared. But three little days ago, she seemed to be at the summit of felicity, and now she was bereaved of every earthly hope. She bore the intelligence of her irreparable loss with astonishing firmness. I did not wonder that she refused to see every human being, for no earthly power

* No doubt the gallantry of every British regiment was equally praiseworthy, but few had such opportunities of displaying it. And we naturally enough heard of the exploits of the brave Highland regiments which had nearly been cut to pieces, and the remains of which, all wounded, had reached Antwerp.

could speak consolation to misery such as hers. In vain I tried to forget her—I could not banish her from my remembrance; and often, during our long wanderings in the distant regions of Holland, when I was far from her, and far from all that might have recalled her to my remembrance, among other sights and other scenes, her early misfortunes wrung my heart with the deepest sorrow.

But whatever might be the grief and anxiety of individuals, the universal joy was unbounded. It is impossible to describe the effects of this victory upon all ranks of people. Every human heart seemed to beat in sympathy; every countenance beamed with joy; every tongue spoke the language of exultation. As the terror and despair of the Belgians had been excessive, their transport was now vehement and overflowing, and their volubility not to be imagined. We went into several shops, and the people, unable to restrain themselves, poured out upon us the fulness of their joy, their astonishment, their gratitude, their admiration, and their praise. Totally forgetful of their interests, they thought not of selling their goods; they thought of nothing—they could do nothing but talk of the battle and the British, and it was with difficulty we could get them to show us what we wanted: nay, more than once we were actually obliged to go away without doing anything, from the impossibility of making them attend to the business of selling and buying.

But sometimes the expression of their feelings was so simple, so natural, and so touching, and there was so much of truth and naïveté, both in their manner and their words, that it was impossible to hear them without emotion. The French they loaded with execrations; and their hatred, their indignation, and their bitter feelings of their wrongs, said more than volumes of eloquence, or even facts could have done, in condemnation of the conduct of their late masters. All the English merchandise, and all colonial produce, imported even before it was decreed to be a crime, were seized, carried from their shops and warehouses, and burnt before their eyes in the Place Verte. No remuneration, no indemnity whatever was given them; and by this single act of wanton tyranny, hundreds of industrious families were reduced to beggary. Heavy exactions and continual contributions were levied, and the weight of these fell upon the most industrious and respectable orders of the people. "All that we had they took," was said again and again to us, "and if we had had thousands more, it would have all gone." They ruined the commerce, the manufactures, the trade of the country, and then they drained the poor inhabitants of their property. They shut up the sources of wealth, and then called on them for money. They blocked up the fountain, and then asked for its waters. Like Egyptian task-masters, they took from them the materials, and then demanded their work. They expected them to make "bricks without straw." The French soldiers lived at free-quarters upon the people, and the Belgic youths were marched away to fight in foreign wars. The oppressed people were subject to the unrestrained rapine and brutal insolence of the French soldiery, of which they durst not complain. It was unsafe even to murmur. Not only the liberty of the press, but the liberty of speech was denied them. Any unfortunate person convicted of holding intercourse with England was imprisoned, and some of them (we were told), by way of example, were shot.

We happened to go into a little stationer's shop, kept by

a widow and her three daughters, who received us almost with adoration because we were English. They all began to talk at once, and relieved their minds by pouring out a torrent of invectives against those detested tyrants, "Ces fléaux du genre humain," as they called them. All their goods had been seized; their shop (which was not then a stationer's) completely stripped of its contents, under the pretence of its being filled with British and colonial produce, which they said was not the case; and a considerable quantity of continental manufactures had also been carried away. "But *that* was nothing," the poor mother said, as she wiped the tears from her eyes, "*that* she could have borne, for though it seemed heavy at the time, she thought less of it now;—but her five sons (fine handsome young men, they were, as ever a mother bore), her five sons were all taken for soldiers, and perished in the French wars; some in the retreat from Russia, and some in the subsequent campaign in Germany." The tears streamed down the cheeks of one of these young women, as she spoke to me of her "poor brothers." I can give no idea of the bitterness, the rancour, the hatred, and above all, the volubility of the abuse which these poor women poured out against the French.

We got away from them with difficulty; and though the deep sense of their own wrongs rankled in their minds, and aggravated the resentment and detestation which they must naturally feel towards the authors of so much misery, yet we found the same sentiments, in greater or in less degree, among all the Belgians with whom we conversed, or whom we heard conversing. I had always understood that the French (and Napoleon in particular) were highly popular in Antwerp, but from some most respectable old-established

merchants, both British and Belgic, we learned that the inhabitants were decidedly hostile to the French, and that they
were both feared and hated by all, excepting the very dregs
of society, and those individuals who had made fortunes
under their administration.

In the course of our rambles we had many conversations
with various people whom we never saw before, and I suppose shall never see again. We met a wounded officer who
had been taken prisoner by the French. He said, that after
repeatedly threatening to kill him, and loading him with
abuse, they actually knocked him on the head with the butt-
end of a musket, and left him for dead upon the field: he
came, however, to himself, and effected his escape. His
face was most frightfully swelled, and so bruised, that it was
every shade of black, and blue, and green; his head was
entirely tied up with white handkerchiefs and bloody bandages, and in my life I never saw a more battered object.
He had his arm in a sling; but he was by much too rejoiced at his escape to care about his wounds or bruises. He
told us, what *then* I could scarcely believe, that the French
had killed many of our officers whom they had taken prisoners, and that they had *piked* numbers of the wounded.
The truth of these brutal murders, disgraceful to humanity,
and even more dishonourable and more barbarous than the
worst cruelty of savages, were unhappily, afterwards, too in-
disputably proved.

In our progress through the streets we could not resist
stopping to speak to such of the poor wounded soldiers as
seemed able to talk, and who looked as if they would thank
us even for a word of kindness, much to the amazement of
Mr. D., an Antwerp merchant, who was walking about with

us, to " show us the lions," as he said. However, he waited most patiently, while Mrs. H., my sister, and I talked to ensigns, sergeants, corporals, and common soldiers, who were all, more or less, wounded or disabled.

" We have got six of those wounded soldiers billeted upon us," said Mr. D., as we walked on, "but I must get them boarded out somewhere, for they would be very troublesome in the house." " Troublesome!" I exclaimed. "Yes! you know they would be very troublesome in a house, though I suppose the surgeons will look after their *wounds,* and all *that* ; they will cost me" (I forget how many guelders he said) "a week, but I would rather *pay* it" (with a strong and proud emphasis upon the word pay) "than have them in the house, it would be so very disagreeable."

I was silent, for I durst not trust myself to speak. Yet this was a very well-meaning man. I make no doubt he subscribed *handsomely* to the Waterloo fund, and that he would have given money to those very wounded soldiers to whom he refused shelter—if he had thought they wanted it. But beyond giving money his ideas of charity did not extend. To his mercantile mind, money was the chief and only good; the sole source of pride and of happiness; the only object in life worth seeking after—the one thing needful. He was a very good kind of man in his way, but he was entirely occupied with his " snug box" at Clapham, his brother's grand potteries in Staffordshire, and his own cargoes of rice, and hogsheads of rum and sugar ; he could not feel the vast debt of gratitude their country owed to " the men of Waterloo;" to those gallant soldiers who had fought and bled for her safety and glory. He did not mean to be unkind or ungenerous ; he would have started at the reproach of wanting humanity, or being deficient in gratitude, but—but—but—in short, he was altogether an Antwerp merchant.

The day was extremely hot, and on the outside of the Cafés, beneath the shade of awnings, and seated beside little tables in the open street, the Belgic gentlemen were eating ces and fruit, and drinking coffee, and reading "L'Oracle de Bruxelles," and playing at domino and backgammon with the utmost composure, utterly regardless of the crowds of passengers, and apparently as much at their ease as if they were in their own houses,—or indeed more so; for the Belgians, like the French, are more at home at le Café, or in the public streets, or anywhere, than in their own home, which is the last place in which they think of looking for enjoyment. They have no notion of domestic comfort, domestic pleasure, or domestic happiness; and consequently they cannot have much knowledge of domestic virtues. I cannot, therefore, help considering the French as a gay, rather than a happy nation. French habits and manners, and, I am afraid, French morals, are universally prevalent throughout Belgium. Groups of ladies of the most respectable character may everywhere be seen, sitting on chairs or benches, in the public streets or promenades, working, talking, laughing, and amusing themselves with all the ease and gaiety and sangfroid in the world. Sometimes only a knot of ladies, but more frequently ladies coquetting with their obsequious beaux.

We visited the unfinished Quay, begun by Napoleon, which was to have extended above a mile along the broad and deep Scheldt, and would have been one of the finest quays in Europe. We saw the flying bridge ("Le Pont

Volant"), a most ingenious contrivance, on which carriages, horses, and waggons pass with great rapidity and security from one side of the river to the other, without interrupting its navigation, even for vessels of the largest burden. Such a plan, I should think, might be adopted with great success upon the Thames between London and Gravesend, or in any river where the arches of a stone bridge would obstruct the passage of the ships, and where the breadth is too great for the single span of an iron bridge. The mechanism seemed to be very simple. The largest ships of war can come up close to the quay; but the navigation of the Scheldt is difficult, and even dangerous, from the number of sand banks which choke it up. Antwerp is upwards of fifty miles from the mouth of the river.

We saw the docks, the offspring of Napoleon's hatred against our country; one of them was made sufficiently large and deep to be capable of containing the greatest part of the British navy, and at one time he exulted in the expectation of seeing the "wooden walls" of Old England safely moored in *his* docks at Antwerp. Little did he anticipate the day when the little army of England, which he despised and ridiculed, should be the unmolested possessors of *his* capital of Paris!

The Arsenal (la Maison de Marine) is now emptied of its stores, and deserted by its workmen. We saw a long building erected by Napoleon for the manufacture of ropes for ships—now equally useless. Its length is precisely the same as that of the cable of a first-rate British ship of war. The manner in which they repair ships in these docks is unlike anything I ever saw before. Instead of lifting the ship entirely out of water, and placing it upon the stocks (in effecting which, or in relaunching it, a vessel is said often to sustain injury), a rope is attached to the masts, and the ship is hauled down until its keel is exposed; after repairing that side they haul it down on the other in the same manner, and the workmen stand upon a raft that is fastened to its side.

We went to see the Citadel, a noble and complete fortification overlooking the Scheldt. The walls are of such an immense height and thickness, that I should imagine them to be quite invulnerable. The fortress is capable of containing 10,000 men; by means of the river fresh reinforcements might be constantly thrown in; and with a strong garrison, and an adequate supply of provisions and ammunition, I should suppose, that like another Troy, it might stand a ten years' siege; only that modern patience would never hold out such a length of time.

The commandant was confined to his bed by indisposition; but every part of the fortification was explained to us by a very good-humoured, intelligent Irish officer, whose name I have forgotten, but who seemed to be excessively amused by the (I fear) almost childish delight which my sister and I betrayed in seeing all the wonders of this wonderful place. Everything to us was new and interesting. It was the first citadel we had ever seen: and to see with our own eyes a real, actual citadel—nay, more, to be in one, was so very delightful, that we both agreed, if we had seen nothing else, we should have thought ourselves amply repaid for our journey to Antwerp.

This good-natured officer contentedly toiled along with us, under the burning rays of a most sultry sun, round the whole foritfications, and pointed out to us where and how attacks might be made with success, and in what manner they could be resisted. The sight of the moat, the draw-bridges, the ramparts, the bastions, and the dungeons; the sally-ports and gates, which communicate with the citadel from the moat by long subterranean passages, so forcibly re-called to my recollection all that I had heard and read of battles and sieges in history and in tales of chivalry, that I could have fancied myself transported back into ages long since past—into the iron times of arms; and all that had before existed only in imagination was at once realised.

After visiting all the lions of Antwerp, docks and for-tresses; and ships and statues, and pictures and prisons; and quays and cathedrals; and battle-beaten walls and flying bridges; and decayed monasteries, and modern arsenals; which, as they have all been often so much better described than I can describe them, I shall forbear to describe at all—we returned to the hotel, excessively heated and tired, and very glad to sit down to rest. To-day, for the first time since our arrival, we began to have serious thoughts of getting some dinner. We might have eaten something during those days of alarm and agitation, and I suppose we did; but, excepting the breakfast we had got upon the stairs at Brus-sels on Saturday, I have not the most distant recollection of ever having eaten at all.

Upon the necessity and expediency of now dining, how-ever, we were all unanimously agreed: the difficulty was how to achieve it. Mr. and Mrs. H. had a pigeon-hole for their only habitation, in which it would have been perfectly impossible to have introduced a table; a single chair was all it was capable of containing. In our rooms we had some difficulty in turning round when more than one person at a time was in them; but by dint of sitting *out* of the window, and against the door, and upon all the boxes, we had, I was assured—for I actually did not re-member it—ingeniously succeeded in getting some breakfast —but to dine was perfectly impracticable. There happened, however, to be in this very hotel, a Captain F., an idle, not a fighting, captain; one who made his campaigns, not at Waterloo, but in Bond-street; and this Captain F., who had been in Antwerp long before the commencement of hostilities, had, luckily for us, got possession of a room in which it was possible to move. He was a Newmarket friend of Mr. H.'s, who introduced him to us, with the recom-mendation that he was a young man of fashion and fortune, well known about town; and in Captain F.'s room and company, Mr. and Mrs. H., my sister, my brother, and I accordingly dined; we were also favoured with the company of a particular friend of his, a Mr. C. Many foolish young men it has been my lot to see, but never did I meet with any whose folly was at all comparable to that of Captain F.

Captain F. was a young man who prided himself upon his knowledge of horse-flesh, and who had, by his own ac-count, been jockeyed out of " many a cool thousand" by his ignorance of it; he was a young man who delighted in building more *new invented* carriages in one year than he could pay for in twenty; he was a young man who prided himself upon borrowing money from Jews at fifteen per cent. while his guardians were saving it for him at five; and in squandering it at Newmarket while they thought him poring over Greek and mathematics at Cambridge; he was a young man whose highest pride consisted in driving four-in-hand " knowingly;" whose greatest ambition was to resemble a stage-coachman exactly, and whose distinguishing characteristic was that of being a most egregious fool.

In consequence, I suppose, of a perseverance in this laudable career, Captain F. now found it more convenient to play the fool upon the continent than in England. After recounting to us various and manifold deeds of folly committed in London and Newmarket, amongst Jews and Whip Clubs, he at length gravely asserted, " that it was impossible for any man to dress under seven hundred a year."

This piece of information was received by some of the party with equal amazement and incredulity : but Captain F. assured us, " 'Pon his soul it was true; that he knew as well as any man what it was to dress, and that it could not be done for less than seven hundred a year—nay, that it often costs nine."

" And pray, Captain F.," said I, involuntarily glancing at his coat, which happened not to be by any means a new one, " do *you* spend nine hundred a year upon dress?" " Oh! not *now*," he exclaimed; " I don't dress *now*; I never dressed but eighteen months in my life." He then explained at large to me, who, in my ignorance, had not understood what to dress meant, " that ' to dress' signified to be the first in fashion, to make it the study of one's life to appear in a'new mode before anybody else; ' to sport' something new every day; and during the time he dressed," he said, " his tailor sent him down three boxes of clothes every week from town, wherever he might happen to be." Having thus satisfactorily proved, that, at a considerable expense to his pocket, he had turned himself into a sort of block for the tailors to attire in their new invented coats and waistcoats, like the wooden dolls the milliners dress up to set off their

new fashions, he next poured out such a quantity of nonsense
about the battle and the wounded, that he reminded me of
Hotspur's account of his interview with a coxcomb of the
same species:

"When the fight was done,——"

But why do I waste a word upon him.

A Scotch acquaintance, Mr. E., of M., arrived this
evening from the field, where he had been ineffectually engaged in the soul-harrowing employment of searching
among the dead, the wounded, and the dying, for his
youngest brother, who was nowhere to be found. He was
a gallant-spirited youth of eighteen, and this was his first
campaign. His horse had returned without its rider—
among the multitude of wounded he could not be found.
Some hopes, some faint hopes, yet remained that he might
have been taken prisoner, and that he might yet appear;
but there was too much reason to fear that he had perished,
though where or how was unknown. Alas! every passing
day made the hopes of his friends more and more improbable. No tidings were ever heard of him, and " on earth he
was seen no more." The uncertainty in which the fate of
this lamented young man was involved was even more
dreadful than the knowledge of the worst could have been.
Mrs. H.'s anxiety respecting her brother was relieved by
Mr. E.'s assurance of his being in perfect safety. He could
tell us nothing of the fate of those for whom we were so
deeply anxious. "Do not ask me," he exclaimed, " who *is*
wounded—I cannot tell you.. It would be easy to say who
are *not*." Intelligence from another quarter, however, relieved our fears, and although it subsequently proved false,

for the present it led us to believe that our friends were in safety.

We now learnt that the battle had been even more desperate, and the victory more glorious and decisive, than Lord Wellington's concise and modest bulletin had led us to imagine. The French had not "retreated," they had been completely routed, and put to flight; they had not merely "been defeated," they were no longer an army. They had fled in every direction from the field, pursued by the victorious British and by the Prussians, who had not come up till just at the close of the battle.* The whole of their artillery, ammunition, and baggage, their caissons, all the matériel of their army had been taken. Of 130,000 Frenchmen who had marched yesterday morning to battle, flushed with all the hopes and confidence of victory, no trace, no vestige now remained; they were all swept away; they were scattered by the whirlwind of war over the face of the earth. Yesterday their proud hosts had spread terror and dismay through nations, and struck consternation into every heart, except those of the brave band of warriors who opposed them. To-day the greater part of them slept in death, the rest were fugitives or captives. It was an awful and tremendous lesson. They were gone with all their imperfections on their heads, —their hopes, their purposes, their plans, their passions, and their crimes, were at rest for ever! And their leader, who had sported away the lives of thousands, with feelings untouched by remorse ; who had impiously presumed to defy the powers of God and man; and whose insatiate ambition the world itself seemed too small to contain—where was he now?—an outcast and a wanderer, hunted, pursued, beset on all sides, and at a loss where to lay his head !

* [See Appendix, B.]

It was with a heart pierced with anguish that I wept for the brave who had fallen ; that I felt in the bitterness of sorrow, that not even the proud triumph of my country's glory could console me for the gallant hearts that were lost to her for ever !

> " How many mothers shall lament their sons;
> How many widows weep their husbands slain!—
> Ye dames of Albion! ev'n for you I mourn:
> Who sadly sitting on the sea-beat shore,
> Long look for lords who never shall return!"

It was twelve o'clock before our friends left us, and then, worn out with fatigue of body and mind, for the first time during four nights, I enjoyed the blessing of some hours of undisturbed repose, in spite of the bonfires, the acclamations, the noisy rejoicings, and the songs, more patriotic than melodious, which resounded in my ears. Last night the streets were filled with the cries of horror and alarm, to-night they resounded with the shouts of exultation and joy ; and it was with feelings of deep and fervent thanksgiving to Heaven that I laid my wearied head upon the pillow, and sank to sleep with the blessed consciousness that we should not this night be disturbed by the dreadful alarms of war.

Nothing on retrospection seemed to me so extraordinary as the shortness of time in which these wonderful events had happened. I could scarcely convince myself that they had actually been comprised in the short space of three days—so long did it seem to be ! Yet in that brief space how many gallant spirits had death arrested in their glorious career of honour and immortality—how many hearts had grief rendered desolate ! In these eventful days the fates of empires and of kings had been decided, and the trembilng nations of Europe freed from the vengeance and the yoke of the tyranny which menaced them with subjugation.

If the passage of time were to be computed by the succession of events, rather than by moments, we should indeed have lived a lifetime! an age! for it was "eternity of thought." Every thing that had happened, even immediately before these events, seemed like the faintly-remembered traces of a dream, or the fading and distant images of long past years. It seemed as if at once

> " From the tablet of my memory
> Were wiped away all trivial fond records,
> All saws of books, all forms, all pressures past,
> That youth and observation copied there;
> And this remembrance all alone remain'd,
> Within the book and volume of my brain,
> Unmixed with baser matter."

Yes! the days, the months, the years of my future life may pass away and be forgotten, and all the changes that mark them fade like a morning dream; but the minutest circumstance of these eventful days must be remembered " while Memory holds her seat;" for such moments and such feelings in life can never return more.

A fortnight elapsed, which we passed in making the tour of Holland; in gliding along its slow canals, visiting its populous cities, gazing at its splendid palaces, yawning over its green ditches, wondering at its great dykes, its prodigious sluices, and its innumerable windmills; admiring its clean houses, laughing at the humours of its fairs, and falling fast asleep in its churches.

We found the Dutch a plain, plodding, pains-taking, well-meaning, money-getting, matter-of-fact people; very dull and drowsy, and slow and stupid; little addicted to talking, but very much given to smoking; but withal pious and chari-

table, and just and equitable ; with no wit, but some humour;
with little fancy, genius, or invention—but much patience,
perseverance, and punctuality.   They make excellent merchants, but very bad companions.   What Buonaparte once
in his ignorance said of the English, is truly applicable to
the Dutch,—" They are a nation of shopkeepers ;" and they
used to remind me very much of a whole people of Quakers.
In dress, in manners, in appearance, and in habits of life,
they precisely resemble that worthy sect; and like them, in
all these points they are perfectly stationary.   It is singular
enough that in all matters of taste and fashion, in which
other nations are continually varying, the Dutch 'have stood
stock still for at least two centuries ; and in political opinions
and institutions, which it requires years, and even ages, to
alter in other countries, the Dutch have veered about without ceasing.   They have literally changed their form of
government much oftener than the cut of their coats.   They
have had Stadtholders, and Revolutions, and Republics, and
Despotisms, and Tyrants, and limited Monarchies ; and new
Dynasties and old; and the " New Code Napoleon,"—and
the newer Code of King William : and they have changed
from the side of England to that of France, and from
France to that of England,—and from the House of Orange
to Buonaparte, and from Buonaparte to the House of Orange,
with a rapidity and versatility which even their volatile
neighbours, the French, could not equal.

But while their government, their laws, their sovereigns,
and their institutions, have undergone every possible trans-
formation—the fashion of their caps and bonnets, their hats
and shoebuckles, remains unchanged ; and they have adhered,
with the most scrupulous exactitude, to the same forms of

politeness, the same hours, dresses, manners, and habits of life that were the fashion among the venerable Burgomasters in the days of good King William. Certainly if Solomon had ever lived in Holland he never would have said that "the fashion of this world passeth away," for there it lasts from generation to generation.

I should think that the Dutch are now very like what the English were in the times of the Puritans. They have a great deal of rigidity and vulgarity in their appearance, and of coarseness and *grossièreté* in their manners; and they are wholly destitute of vivacity, refinement, and "the grace that charms." I speak of the people at large; not of the Court nor of the courtly, who in every country are much the same, or at least fashioned upon one model; but, excepting the Court, there is no polite circle, no general good society. It is the rarest thing in the world to meet with a gentleman in Holland. The Dutch are equally devoid of that acquired good breeding which distinguishes the well educated English, and that native politeness and winning courtesy which is so irresistibly engaging among the French, and even the Belgic people.

I did not think anything could have roused the phlegmatic Dutch to such energy and vehement animation as they showed in their ardent attachment to the present government, and their detestation of their former tyrants. They are absolutely enthusiastic in their loyalty to the House of Orange; and their implacable and virulent hatred to the French surpasses all conception. They cannot be silent upon this subject; they cannot forget their past sufferings, and the tyranny and cruelty which they endured so long.

H

They never utter their names without bitter execrations, and the very language is become unpopular. But the British they look upon with the highest respect and admiration, and treat them with a blunt, coarse, complimentary sort of kindness, which is flattering to our national pride.

The Dutch, however, allowed that Louis Buonaparte was a very well-intentioned, good-hearted man; but he was only a tool in the hands of the " Great Napoleon;" and, though he did not like to crush them, he had no power to mitigate the tyranny which bowed them to the earth. For Napoleon himself—his ministers, his soldiers, his edicts, and the system of plunder, oppression, and slavery which constituted his government—no words are strong enough to speak their abhorrence. They are now most completely an unanimous people. From the lowest beggar in the street to the king upon his throne, one common political feeling animates and inspires them.

The only people who grew rich during the reign of the French were the smugglers, and some of these men made astonishing fortunes by the sale of colonial produce,—chiefly coffee and tobacco; and English manufactures, which they introduced into the kingdom in great quantities, notwithstanding all the spies, soldiers, plans, penalties, and prohibitions of Buonaparte.

In the failure of taxes and contributions to satisfy his rapacity, he sequestrated a large portion of the funds destined for the annual repair of the dykes and sluices, which in consequence were fast falling to decay; so that had the French Government lasted much longer, Holland might have been no longer a country; it might *physically*, as well as *politically*, have ceased to exist, and a tide, even more destructive than the armies of France, have rolled over it and restored it again to the ocean.

Sometimes the faint reports of distant war roused us during our slumbering progress through this soporific country; and Dutch men and Dutch bonnets, and towns and palaces, and universities and museums, and tulips and hyacinths, and even "Orange Boven" itself, were entirely forgotten in the animating and overpowering interest of the triumphant progress of the British arms,—the final fall of the Usurper of France,—and the entrance of the Allied Army, led by the Duke of Wellington, into the gates of Paris.

A sight more affecting than any other that Holland contained we frequently witnessed:—long *treckschuyts* filled with the wounded Dutch soldiers of Waterloo, mutilated, disabled, sick and suffering, passed us upon the canals, slowly returning to their homes. In many of the towns and villages of Holland, the hospitals were filled with these poor soldiers, to whom the inhabitants showed the most humane and praiseworthy kindness and attention. It is but justice to the Dutch to state, that though their charity began at home it did not end there. Every town and village made contributions for the wounded Belgic and British, as well as for the Dutch, both of money and provisions, including plenty of butter and cheese, together with an enormous supply of ankers of real Hollands, which amused me extremely. I am sure they sent it out of pure love and kindness, anxious, I suppose, that the poor wounded should have plenty of what they liked best themselves; or perhaps they thought that gin, like spermaceti, was "sovereign for an inward bruise."

If Ireland be " the country that owes the most to Nature

and the least to Man," Holland is unquestionably the country
which owes the most to Man and the least to Nature. I
bade it farewell without one feeling of regret: with as little
emotion as Voltaire, I could have said—" Adieu! Canaux,
Canards, Canaille!"—and after crossing many a tedious and
toilsome ferry, and slowly traversing the trackless and sandy
desert which separates Bergen-op-Zoom from Antwerp, we
left Holland,—I hope, for ever!

Nothing can be imagined more dreary than this journey.
One wide extended desert of barren sand surrounded us as
far as the eye could reach, in which no trace of man, nor
beast, nor human habitation, could be seen. Some bents,
thinly scattered upon the hillocks of sand, and occasional
groups of stunted fir, through which the wind sighed mournfully, were the only signs of vegetation. Slowly and heavily
the horses dragged our cabriolet through these deep sands,
choosing their own path as their own sagacity, or that of
their driver, directed. Quitting at last this solitary waste,
we entered the sheltering copse woods of oak which surround
the city of Antwerp, drove swiftly by neat cottages and
smiling gardens, descried with delight its lofty walls, its
frowning fortifications, and the spire of the Cathedral, whose
beauty we could *now* admire; and with feelings which may
be better conceived than described, we once more entered
its gates.—But what a change had one fortnight produced!
It did not seem to be the same place or the same people;
and when I thought of all the quick varying scenes of horror,
consternation, and triumph which we had witnessed here,
and remembered that within these walls we had trembled
for the safety, and mourned the imaginary defeat of that
army who were now victorious in the capital of France;
when I recalled all that the heroes of my country had done

and dared and suffered for her honour and security and peace—and that to them, under Heaven, Europe owed its salvation—it was difficult, it was nearly impossible to restrain the strong tide of mingled emotions which at this moment swelled my heart. Not for worlds, not to have been the first and greatest in another land, would I have resigned the distinction of calling England my country; and I blessed Heaven that I was born an Englishwoman, and born in this, the proudest era of British glory.

As these reflections rapidly passed through my mind, a Highland soldier obstructed our passage with his musket, signifying to the driver that he was to go at a foot-pace past a large building, which we now discovered to be an hospital, and before which the street was thickly laid with straw. We were affected with this proof of the attention and care paid to the wounded, still more so when we learnt that this hospital was full of wounded French. The Highland soldier who now stood on guard to prevent the smallest noise from disturbing the repose of his enemies, had himself been wounded—wounded in the action with them. It was a noble, a divine instance of generosity: it was returning good for evil. It was worthy of England. The French soldiers had inhumanly murdered their wounded prisoners. The British not only dressed the wounds and attended to all the wants of theirs, but they protected and watched over them, that even their very slumbers might not be disturbed.

At the hotel of Le Grand Laboureur they knew and welcomed us again, and testified great joy at the success of the Allies since we had seen them, and a great dread lest Napoleon should make his escape. In the streets we met numbers of poor wounded British officers, weak, pale, faint, and emaciated, slowly and painfully moving a few yards to taste the freshness of the summer and the blessed beams of heaven.

Many fine young men had lost their limbs, many were on crutches, many were supported by their wives or by their servants. At the open windows of the houses, propped up by pillows, some poor unfortunate sufferers were lying, whose looks would have moved a heart of stone to pity. We passed several hospitals, and looked into some of them. The cleanliness and neatness of appearance which they exhibited were truly gratifying.

Antwerp was filled with wounded. In every corner we met numbers of convalescent soldiers and officers, some of whom looked well; but the sufferings we saw, and heard of, were far too dreadful to relate, and in many cases death would have been a blessed relief from a state of hopeless torture. Several vessels had already sailed, filled with convalescent wounded, for England.

Most of the wounded French, the wretched survivors of Buonaparte's imperial army, were here. But what consolation had they to support them on the bed of pain and sickness? What glory awaited them when they returned to their native country? What was their recompense for their valour, their sufferings, their services, and their dangers?—Broken health, and blighted hopes, and ruined fortunes, and blasted fame, were all they had to look to. They had not fought and bled for their country, but for a leader who had basely deserted them. Surrounded by these bleeding victims of a tyrant's ungovernable ambition, I felt the truth that inspired the poet's lines—

"Unblest is the blood that for tyrants is squandered,
And Fame has no wreath for the brow of the slave."

And what British heart would not exclaim with him—

"But hail to thee, Albion, who meet'st the commotion
Of Europe, as firm as thy cliffs meet the foam,
With no bond but the law, and no slave but the ocean—
Hail, Temple of Liberty! thou art my home!"

The night soon closed in upon us, and we could see the wounded no more. We went to rest, and enjoyed a night of more calm repose than it had ever yet been our lot to experience in Antwerp.

With what different feelings, and under what different circumstances, did I open my eyes on this Sunday morning, to those which we suffered on the dreadful morning of Sunday, the 18th of June, which we had spent here before! Then horror and despair filled the minds of the people— then they were lamenting the imaginary destruction of that army for whose success they were now offering up thanks— for this was the *Kennesgevin*, or day of thanksgiving, for the glorious victory of Waterloo. We attended high mass at the Cathedral, as we had done before—but with sensations how different! and if at that awful moment my prayers had ascended to heaven, to crown with victory and glory the arms of my country, the deep and fervent emotions of gratitude which filled my heart were now offered up in thanksgiving to the throne of divine mercy. The anxiety, the misery that I had endured when I was before within these aisles, was too poignant to be easily forgotten; but that remembrance made me feel more deeply the blessings which Heaven had bestowed upon us.

Mass being over, we ascended by 640 steps to the top of the tower, or rather of the staircase, of the Cathedral, for its utmost pinnacle is accessible only to the winged inhabitants of air: but as we were not furnished with wings, we were

obliged to content ourselves, instead of soaring higher, with
gazing upon the magnificent prospect that lay below us.
The men and women flocking out of the churches through
the streets, looked exactly like a colony of ants swarming on
the gravel walks of a garden in a sunny day: the streets and
houses looked like the miniature model of a town in pasteboard; and the majestic Scheldt like a long ribbon stream-
ing through a measureless tract of country.

However, the view was both various and beautiful. Far
as the eye could reach, the rich fields and woods of Flanders, with its populous villages, its lofty spires, and noble
canals lay extended around us, presenting a striking contrast
to the cold, bare, triste, watery flats of Holland, which were
fresh in our remembrance; and Flanders, no doubt, looked
doubly beautiful from the recent comparison.

We distinctly saw the fortifications of Bergen-op-Zoom on
one side, and the steeple of Vilvorde on the other. We
traced the Scheldt winding its course through a rich country
down towards the ocean. Upon its broad bosom lay the vessels waving with the flag of Britain, and destined to carry
home the troops who had so bravely fought and bled in her
service, and for her glory.

When I thought of the dreadful waste of human life and
sufferings which the battle of Waterloo had cost the world,
it almost seemed as if it had been dearly purchased: yet in
frequent indecisive battles, and in long-protracted campaigns, more blood might—must have been shed, without the
same glorious or important results.   In one great day, years of
bloodshed and of toil had been saved.   In one tremendous
burst of thunder the war had ended, and the lightnings of
Heaven in that vengeful hour had descended upon the head

of the guilty. The dark cloud which menaced Europe had passed away, and the prospect was now calm, bright, and unclouded. The blood of Britons had indeed flowed, but it had flowed in a noble cause, and it had not flowed in vain. It had secured present peace and security to the world, and it had left to future ages the proudest monument of British fame.

But I forget that I am all this time upon the top of Antwerp Cathedral; and it is high time to descend from my altitude. When we once more reached the earth, we went to see a sort of religious puppet-show, called Mount Calvary. It had been "got up" with great care and cost, and must have required a world of labour; for there were artificial rocks and caverns, and heaven and hell into the bargain; and it was altogether a most edifying spectacle. There were the Crucifixion, and the Virgin Mary, and St. Paul, and St. Peter,—and I dare say all the rest of the Apostles, and at least fifty more holy persons, who were most likely saints, all as large as life, and made of white stone. There were also red-hot flaming furnaces of purgatory, filled with figures of the same materials; with this difference, that they were making horrible grimaces. There were also the Sepulchre and the Angel; and our friend Mr. D. (the Antwerp merchant), who took us to see this show, was in an ecstasy with it, and declared that all the paintings in the world were not to be compared to it—nay, that he did actually think that it was almost as well worth seeing as St. Paul's or the Monument; —but this he asserted more cautiously.

We visited the house and the tomb of Rubens with more veneration than we had paid to the shrines of all the saints. The people of Antwerp almost adore the memory of this great artist. He was descended from one of the most ancient families in Flanders; of noble birth and of splendid fortune. Antwerp was the place of his birth and of his death, and his spirit still seems to hover over it; for never did I witness a passion for paintings, and a knowledge of the art, so universally diffused among all classes as in this town. All the merchants, and even the petty shopkeepers and tradespeople, have good paintings, both of the Flemish and Italian school. In every house they may be seen; and in every street even the lowest of the people may be heard to canvass their merits. They still lament over the loss of the fine paintings which were carried from the churches by the French; and they seemed particularly to grieve for their celebrated Altarpiece, the pride of their city, which was taken from them. They petitioned and implored Buonaparte with so much importunity and perseverance to restore to them this idol of their affections, that he at last promised it should be sent back. In process of time, and in conformity with his imperial word, there arrived the celebrated altar-piece of " The Descent from the Cross,"—correctly copied from the original by a modern French artist! The immortal touches of Rubens were not there. The fraud was instantly discovered, and the people were indignant at this mockery of restitution. They told us they intended immediately to send deputies to Paris to claim this and the other treasures of which they had been despoiled, and which now adorn the Louvre.

There are some very fine private cabinets of pictures in Antwerp, which are opened to strangers with all that alacrity and politeness which in England, in such cases, we are so lamentably and notoriously deficient in. In one of these we saw the celebrated " Chapeau Pâle " of Rubens. I was disappointed in it; probably from having had my expectations too highly raised by hearing its beauties extravagantly extolled. In fact, the subject does not call forth any great powers either of genius or execution. It is simply the portrait of a handsome woman with a very attractive countenance, and dressed in a very becoming grey beaver hat and feather; and both the lady and her hat are most beautifully painted. We saw some landscapes by Rubens, some of which were very fine. There is no branch of painting which the versatile genius of this wonderful man did not lead him to attempt, and none in which he did not succeed. His Scriptural and historical paintings, upon which rests his fame; his allegories, portraits, and landscapes, are well known: but I have seen a miniature picture of his performance, beautifully finished—a piece of fruit and flowers, very well executed, though in an uncommon style—and lastly, *an interior*, not a servile copy of Teniers, Ostade, or Gerard Douw, but marked with his own characteristic originality of manner and expression. This last piece is in the possession of a Flemish gentleman at Ghent.

At Antwerp we saw some beautiful landscapes by Asselins and Dietrichsen; a very fine Holy Family by Murillo; and the Death of Abel by Guido. The whole figure of Abel prostrate on the earth, but especially the touching, the more than human expression of his face as he looks up at his brother and his murderer, is one of the finest things I ever beheld in painting. It is in that upward look of pathetic supplication and unutterable feeling that Guido is unrivalled —it is his characteristic excellence. We saw some very fine paintings both by Italian and Flemish artists, but the fascination of the former, in spite of myself, riveted my eyes upon their never-satiating beauties. It is impossible not to feel the decided superiority of the Italian over the Flemish school of painting, in force, delicacy, and dignity of expression; in the power of transposing *soul* into painting, if I may so express myself, and in all that constitutes the greatness and the sublimity of the art. But the Flemish artists laboured under great natural disadvantages. They did not live beneath the brilliant sky that sheds its tints of beauty over the happier climates of Italy and Provence ; they did not dwell in the enchanting vales and sunny mountains, or gaze upon the caverned rocks and romantic solitudes which formed and perfected the genius of a Claude Lorraine, Vernet, Salvator Rosa, and Poussin. Fate threw Berghem and Both, and Cuyp, under unkinder skies, and amidst less picturesque scenes ; but in genius they are perhaps equal, if not superior, to the French and Italian masters. Nor were Rubens, Rembrandt, Teniers, and many of the Flemish artists, inferior to any in conception and execution, in originality, in invention, in truth of expression, and all the natural and acquired powers which constitute the perfection of the painter's art. And if the Italian artists—if Guido, Raphael, Buonarotti, Carlo Dolce, and Correggio, possess a pathos and sublimity, a force, a grace, and an undefinable charm of expression, which makes their works unequalled on earth—let it be remembered that the Flemish artists did not, like them, wake to life amidst the beauty and the harmony of nature; they were not surrounded by faces and forms of speaking, moving expression—of heavenly sublimity and soul-subduing tenderness. The "human face divine" was not moulded of the finer elements of beauty and of grace.—Painting is an imitative art. The world which Nature had spread before them they copied, but they could not create a new one. They were driven to seek in the habitations of men for the sources of that interest which the scenes of Nature denied them; and their powerful and original genius, seizing upon the materials which surrounded them, formed for itself a new and distinct school. They were most faithful copies of Nature. It is impossible to travel through Belgium and Holland and not notice at every step the landscapes of Hobbima, the *Interiors* of Ostade and Gerard Douw; the faces, figures, and humorous scenes which Teniers has exhibited so often to our view; and to recognise at every turn the fat and fair, and well-fed and well-clad beauties of F. Mieres. But the paintings and the painters of Italy and Flanders have led me far from my travels. To return to Antwerp.

After the bright-painted, well-scoured, baby-house looking towns of Holland, the streets of Antwerp appeared very grand and magnificent, but extremely dirty. Remarking this to an English, or rather an Irish officer, he laughed, and said they were beautifully clean in comparison of the state in which the British troops found them when they first came to the garrison. Their complaints of the filthiness and unwholesomeness of the town produced no effect; and to their representations of the necessity of cleaning it, the magistrates answered, with offended dignity, that " the city of Antwerp *was* clean." The British commandant then ordered our soldiers to sweep the streets, and to pile up all the dirt against the houses of those magistrates who with so much pertinacity maintained that the city of Antwerp was clean! The mountains of dirt collected by the soldiers in one morning blocked up the windows, and it was with difficulty that the magistrates could get out of their doors.

When they did, however, they immediately bestirred themselves, convinced by more senses than one that the city of
Antwerp was *not* clean; and they have taken due care ever
since that the streets shall be regularly swept.

The churches in Antwerp were once extremely rich in
silver shrines, images, ornaments, gold plate, and precious
stones; but these treasures, the Belgians said, had been
carried off by Buonaparte: upon more strict inquiry, we
found that these alleged robberies of Napoléon le Grand had
been committed eighteen years ago, most probably by the
sacrilegious hands of the Jacobin Revolutionists, who would
leave little or nothing for imperial plunder. On my remarking this to one of the Belgians, he said, with a shrug of the
shoulder, " Ah! c'est égal—ces gens-là étoient tous les
mêmes—les coquins!" — but whatever mischief has been
done, they always lay it upon Buonaparte, whom they hate
with a bitterness surpassing all conception.

The journey betwixt Antwerp and Brussels was quite new
to us. The anxiety and agitation of mind which we had
suffered on the day we left Brussels for Antwerp, had so
completely engrossed every faculty, that the scenery on the
way had not made the smallest impression on us. The objects of living interest, with which the road was then crowded,
had alone fixed our attention. I could scarcely believe that
I had ever travelled this road before, or ever seen the towns
and villages through which we had so lately passed.

I beheld the same harvest, which I then feared would be
reaped in blood, ripening, to crown the hopes of the husbandman, beneath the blessing of Heaven. My eye now
rested with delight upon the corn fields, waving in rich
luxuriance, the deep verdure of the meadows, and the lofty

woods which diversified the prospect:—the peaceful and prosperous appearance of the country, and the contented, gladsome faces of the people, as they stood at their cottage-doors, "gay in their Sunday 'tire," presented a happy contrast to the terrors and sufferings we had witnessed, and the still more dreadful and multiplied horrors which then seemed ready to burst upon this devoted country.

We entered Malines; but I did not retain the smallest recollection of it until we again reached the inn. From the inn-window I well remembered sorrowfully gazing into the market-place below, and contemplating the train of baggage-waggons, the confusion of English carriages, the parties of troops advancing, the wounded soldiers returning, and the affrighted countenances of the poor Belgic peasantry, crowding together in dismay, with which it was then filled. Now I beheld a very different scene:—a crowd of Belgians, indeed, filled the market-place, but it was a joyous, not a trembling crowd. The people were all amusing themselves after their own fashion. Some flocking to the Church ; others gazing at a wonderful puppet-show, which was stationed at the very door; others listening to a Belgic ballad-singer, who was roaring out, in no very harmonious strains, the downfal of Napoleon, and the warlike prowess of the Belgians; and others were talking and laughing with most noisy glee. The sounds of innocent mirth and pious gratitude were indeed a blessed contrast to the terrors and anxiety we had before witnessed here.

The *Kennesgevin*, or thanksgiving, for the victory, and for the deliverance of the country, had been celebrated, and one priest mounting the pulpit after another, continued to preach a succession of homilies to the people, who might listen to as many or as few of them, as their piety or their taste dictated. We saw a young priest mount the pulpit, and some of the congregation, who had been assembled during the sermon of his predecessor, remained to hear him. He preached in the Belgic language, therefore we could not understand him ; his discourse was apparently extempore, and accompanied with much ungraceful gesticulation. In distant parts of the Church, before the shrine of many a saint, numbers of pious votaries of both sexes were kneeling in silence; engaged in their private earnest devotions, without attending at all to the lectures of the priest, or being disturbed by those who, like us, were wandering up and down the long-drawn aisles and decorated chapels of this ancient Cathedral.

There is a perpetual going in and out, and moving backwards and forwards, during the whole service of the Roman Catholic Church abroad. The people, as soon as they have finished their own prayers, walk off without ceremony, and are succeeded by others ; which in a Protestant church we should think a most scandalous proceeding ; and indeed the service of the Roman Catholic Church itself, both in England and in Ireland, is conducted in a very different manner. It is a common practice here, as well as in France and Italy, for strangers to walk about and examine the churches, paintings, &c., when the Mass is performing ; nor does it seem to annoy the congregation in the least.

The Roman Catholic is the exclusive religion of Belgium . no other form of worship or religious persuasion seems to have any proselytes ; indeed, it is only in consequence of a law enacted since the present King ascended the throne, that other religions have been tolerated. The Belgians are very pious, and even bigoted; but they are not gloomy, they are lively bigots; apparently without a doubt to disturb the fulness of their faith; strict in their observances, gay in their lives, happy in the consolation their religion gives them here, and in its promises hereafter. Comparing their character with that of their unbelieving neighbours, the French, I have no hesitation in preferring bigotry to infidelity. Even the extreme of superstition is better than the horrors of irreligion and atheism.

The Church of Malines is a fine old structure: the towers (for there are two) seem to have been built at an earlier period than the body. We were astonished at the magnificence of the interior. Its magnitude, its antiquity, its lofty arches, its massive pillars, its rich altars, its sculptured figures, and its carved confessionals, have a very imposing effect; and the large, though not fine paintings which adorn its walls, and the decorations which piety has profusely spread over every part of this vast edifice, gave it an air of great splendour. Foreign churches possess a decided advantage, to the eye of the mere spectator, over those of England, from being wholly unincumbered with pews, which certainly take from the grandeur and unity of the whole.

The pulpit of carved wood in this Church is most beautifully executed. It was done only a few years ago by a Flemish artist. There are a few pieces of sculpture of ancient date carved in wood in basso relievo, and painted white, which I admired extremely. The expression given to some of the figures and faces is quite astonishing.

We passed through Vilvorde, half-way to Brussels, where there is a strong *Maison de force* for the imprisonment and employment of criminals. At the little inn where we had

I

before baited our horses, we stopped once more for the same
purpose.   The garçon remembered us immediately, and with
a countenance of great glee expressed his delight to see us
again, and described most vividly the distress they had experienced, and all the rapid and dreadful alarms that had succeeded to each other.   He then reminded us of our parting
prophecy, that the Allies would be victorious, and that the
French would never more penetrate into Flanders, and he
said, he had often thought of it since; and that it had proved
true, for they had indeed seen no French, except " les François blessés."

We proceeded on our journey through a country still im-
proving in beauty.   Sloping grounds, and woods and lawns,
and country seats and pleasure-grounds, and meadows covered
with the richest verdure, greeted our eyes as we advanced to
Brussels.   We met and passed several of the Diligences;
tremendous machines in size, and in slowness, not unlike the
vehicles which in England are used for the conveyance of
wild beasts from one town to another.   They were filled with
an innumerable motley multitude, some of which were playing upon the fiddle, others singing, and all merry-making,
as they jogged along.   The road was much cut up with the
passage of commissariat-waggons, long trains of which we
frequently met upon the way.

We drew near to Brussels, and traversed the margin of
that calm and quiet canal, which, when we left it, had presented a scene of such horrid confusion; and as we approached Lacken we looked up at it once more, but with
very different feelings to those with which we had gazed at
it when we had passed it before, and recollected the boast
Napoleon had made the preceding day—" To-morrow I shall

sleep at Lacken." It was from hence that his premature pompous declarations to the Belgic people were dated, announcing victory; which were even found ready printed in his carriage at Charleroi, after his defeat and flight on the 18th of June.

We entered a sort of wood. On each side of us, upon the grass and beneath the shade of the trees, there was a large encampment of tents, men, horses, waggons, huts, and arms; with all the accompaniments and confusion attendant upon such an establishment. It formed, however, a picturesque and animated scene; fires were burning, suppers cooking, men sleeping, children playing, women scolding, horses grazing, and waggons loading; while long carts and tumbrils were drawn up beneath the trees; parties of Flemish drivers sitting on the ground round the fires, drinking and smoking; and people moving to and fro in every direction. This encampment belonged to the Commissariat department.

We passed the Allée Verte, usually the fashionable promenade for carriages on Sunday evening; but though this was Sunday evening, it was entirely deserted. The inhabitants of Brussels had not yet, perhaps, resumed their habits of gaiety, and in fact the Allée Verte was nearly impassable, owing to the heavy rains and the immense passage of military carriages upon it.

We entered Brussels about the same hour that we had entered it for the first time. Then, the British military were crowding every street; standing at every corner; leaning out of every window, in the full vigour of youth and hope and expectation: then, they were gaily talking and laughing, unconscious that to many it was the last night of their lives. Now, Brussels was filled with the wounded. It is impossible

to describe with what emotions we read the words "Militaires
blessés" marked upon every door; "un, deux, trois, quatre,"
even "huit Officiers blessés," were written upon the houses
in white chalk.   As we slowly passed along, at every open
window we saw the wounded, "languid and pale, the ghosts
of what they were."   In the Parc, which had presented so
gay a scene on the night of our arrival, crowded with
military men, and with fashionable women, a few officers,
lame, disabled, or supported on crutches, with their arms in
slings, or their heads bound up, were now only to be seen,
slowly loitering in its deserted walks, or languidly reclining
on its benches.   The Place Royale, which we had left a
dreadful scene of tumult and confusion, was now quite quiet,
and nearly empty.   It was in all respects a melancholy
contrast, and it was with saddened hearts that we alighted
at the Hôtel de Flandre, where they gladly received us
again, and talked much of the eventful scenes that had followed our departure.

Colonel M., of the Inniskillen Dragoons, was in this hotel.
He had been severely wounded in five different places; he
passed the night after the battle on the road between
Waterloo and Brussels, which was completely blocked up from
the excessive confusion occasioned by the abandoned baggage
and waggons. Although his life had been despaired of, he was
now recovering, and supposed to be out of danger.   Some
English newspapers, which we borrowed, were indescribably
interesting to us; every particular relative to the battle we
read, or rather devoured, with insatiable avidity; but the
list of the killed and wounded we could not get a sight of
till the next morning.   Secure that none of our own friends
were contained in it, we restrained our impatience and went

to rest. Little did we know the shock that awaited us! the misery of the following morning, when we saw the name of Major L. among the list of severely wounded ; and found him at last in a state of extreme suffering and danger ! The days of deep anxiety and individual grief that fol. lowed I pass over in silence. Nor can I bear to dwell upon the miseries it was our lot to witness ; the still more excruciating and hopeless sufferings which we daily heard related, and the scenes of death and distracting affliction which surrounded us. How often was the anxious inquiry made with trembling eagerness for a wounded friend or relation—"Where is he to be found?" How often, after a few minutes of torturing suspense, was the dreadful answer returned—"Dead of his wounds!" Numbers of the young and the brave, after languishing for weeks in hopeless agony, expired during our stay in Brussels ; and it happened more than once within our own knowledge, that the parents, whose earthly hopes and happiness were centred in an only son, arrived from England to see their wounded boy the very day of his decease—in time to gaze upon his insensible and altered corpse, and to follow the mortal remains of all they loved to the grave. The heart-broken countenance, and the silent, motionless grief of one old man, whom I saw under this dreadful affliction, made an impression on my mind too strong to be easily forgotten. Despair seemed to have settled upon his soul, but he neither shed a tear, nor uttered a complaint. I could not even go from the hotel where we stayed to the house where Major L. lodged, without passing crowded hospitals, filled with many hundreds of poor wounded soldiers; and although every attention that skill and humanity could

suggest to contribute to their recovery was paid to them, both
by the British Government and the Belgic people, their
sufferings were dreadful. Many of the British officers died
in the common hospitals: they had been originally conveyed
to them, and it was afterwards found impossible to remove
them.

At every corner the most pitiable objects struck one's
eye. I could not pass through a single street without
meeting some unfortunate being, the very sight of whose
sufferings wrung my heart with anguish. Numbers of
young officers, in the very flower of life and vigour, pale,
feeble, and emaciated, were slowly dragging along their
mutilated forms. Upon couches, supported by pillows, near
the open windows, numbers lay to enjoy the fresh summer
air, and divert the sense of pain by looking at what passed
in the streets. But we knew too well, that the sufferings
we saw were nothing to those we did not see. Every house
was filled with wounded British officers; and how many,
like our old friend Major L., were silently enduring lingering and excruciating torture, unable to raise themselves
from the couch of pain!

Often, as I gazed at the soldier's frequent funeral as it
passed along, I could not help thinking that, though no eye
here was moistened with a tear, yet in some remote cottage
or humble dwelling of my native country, the heart of the
wife or the mother would be wrung with despair for the
loss of him who was now borne unnoticed to a foreign grave.
But let me not dwell upon these scenes of misery; their
remembrance is still too painful—though it can never be
erased from my mind.

When at last we had the consolation of seeing our good old friend out of immediate danger, we dedicated one day to a visit to Waterloo.*

On the morning of Saturday the 15th of July, we set off to visit the field of the ever-memorable and glorious battle of Waterloo. After passing the ramparts, we descended to the pretty little village of Ixelles, embosomed in woods and situated close to the margin of a still, glassy piece of water. From thence we ascended a steep hill, and immediately entered the deep shades of the forest of Soignies, which extends about nine miles from Brussels. The morning was bright and beautiful; the summer sun sported through the branches which met above our heads, and gleamed upon the silver trunks of the lofty beech trees. On either side woodland roads continually struck in various directions through the forest; so seldom trodden, that they were covered with the brightest verdure. At intervals, neat white-washed cottages, and little villages by the roadside, enlivened the forest scenery. We passed through " Vivi-

---

* The road from Brussels to the field of battle was not for some time considered safe, on account of the number of deserters who had taken shelter in the woods, and issued forth, sometimes alone, and sometimes in a gang, to rob passengers and plunder the defenceless cottages and farmhouses of the surrounding country. Neither property nor life certainly could be considered safe at the mercy of these armed desperadoes; but I never heard of any well-authenticated murder that they committed: and from all the inquiries I made, I believe that most of the horrible stories we heard of their enormities were entirely devoid of truth; and that the mischief, even in the way of plunder, they did, was very much exaggerated. Even at the time we went to the field, great apprehensions were entertained by many people of these lawless deserters. Large parties of these were brought in two or three times a week, during our stay in Brussels. They consisted of Belgic, Nassau, and Brunswick soldiers. There was some difficulty in procuring proper places of confinement for them. They were generally sent to the neighbouring Maisons de Force; what eventually was to be their punishment, or what has been their fate, I have never been able to learn.

dolles," "La Petite Espinette," "La Grande Espinette," "Longueville," and several other hamlets whose names I have forgotten.*

Upon the doors of many of the cottages we passed, were written, in white chalk, the names of the officers who had used them for temporary quarters on their way to the battle; or who had been carried there for shelter in returning, when wounded and unable to proceed further. Many we knew had died in these miserable abodes; but all the survivors, excepting one or two of the most severely wounded, had now been removed to Brussels. It was impossible to retrace, without emotion, the very road by which our brave troops had marched out to battle, three weeks before, and by which thousands had been brought back, covered with wounds, in pain and torture. They alone of all that gallant army had returned; thousands had met a glorious death upon the field of battle, and the victorious survivors had pursued their onward march to the capital of France.

I could not help asking myself, as we proceeded along, what would have been the consequences if the French and British armies had happened to encounter each other in the midst of this forest, instead of meeting, as they did, a few miles beyond it? Had our troops been a little later in leaving Brussels on the morning of the 16th of June, this must inevitably have been the case; for it was impossible that the advanced guard of Belgic troops, which was stationed at the outpost of Quatre Bras, could have sustained

---

* It is remarkable that every village in this part of the country has a French name, except Waterloo, which is pronounced by the natives— according to the fashion of the London Cockneys—*Vaterloo;* the letter W being the exclusive property of the British people—with the exception of the aforesaid Cockneys, who resign all claim to it.

the attack of the French, or have delayed their progress for any length of time. But if the hostile armies had encountered each other here, it would have been impossible that a general action could have taken place; the thick entangled underwood makes all entrance into the forest impracticable; and if they had attempted to fight, the road would soon have been choked up with dead. Yet the English, I imagine, would not have retreated, since, if they had, they must either have abandoned Brussels to the enemy, or fought under its very walls; and whether the French would have retreated till they came to open ground, or how they would have manœuvred in such a situation, it was impossible for an unmilitary head like mine even to form a conjecture. During the battle, all the cottages and villages by the wayside had been deserted by their inhabitants, who fled in consternation into the woods, in expectation of the victory and immediate advance of the French, from whom they looked for no mercy. The road had been so dreadfully cut up with the heavy rains and the incessant travelling upon it, that notwithstanding three weeks of summer weather had now elapsed since the battle, the chaussée in the centre was worn into ruts upon the hard pavement, and in many places it was still so deep, that the horses could scarcely drag us through; the unpaved way on each side of the chaussée was perfectly impassable. Along the whole way, shattered wheels and broken remains of waggons still lay, buried among the mud. Their demolition was one of the many consequences that resulted from the violent panic with which the men who were left in charge of the baggage were seized towards the close of the battle. It was originally caused, I understood, by the Belgic cavalry, great numbers of whom fled in the heat of the des-

perate attack made by the French upon our army in front of
Mont St. Jean before the Prussians came up. They were
rallied and brought back by some British officers; but,
unable to stand the dreadful onset of the French, they
turned about again and fled in irretrievable confusion,
trampling upon the wounded and the dying in their speed,
and spreading the alarm that the battle was lost. With
troops less steady, with any other troops, in short, than the
British, the example of flight, joined to such an alarm, at
this critical moment, might have occasioned the loss of the
battle in reality. The men stationed in the rear in charge of
the baggage, who knew nothing of what was going forward,
believed at once the report, and, without stopping a moment
to ascertain its truth, they set off at full speed. If the battle
was lost, it was clearly their business to run away, and they
could not be accused of neglecting this part of their duty.
Following the example of the Belgians, they all set off full
gallop in the utmost confusion, pell-mell, along the road to
Brussels. Nothing is so infectious, nothing so rapid in its
progress as fear: the panic increased every moment; the
terrified fugitives overtook the carts filled with wounded,
and encountered waggons and troops, and military supplies
coming up to the field. It was impossible to pass: the road,
confined on each side by the thickly woven and impenetrable
underwood, was speedily choked up; those who were proceeding to the army insisted upon going one way, and those
who were running away from it, persisted in going the other.
The confusion surpassed all description; till at last, amidst
the crash of waggons, the imprecations of the drivers, and
the cries of the soldiers, a battle took place, and many were
the broken heads and bruises, and various were the wounds

and contusions received in this inglorious fray. It is even said, and I fear with truth, that some lives were lost. The baggage was abandoned, and scattered along the road; the waggons were thrown one upon another into the woods, and over the banks by the road-side; the horses, half-killed, were left to perish; and the wounded were deserted. Over every obstacle these panic-struck people, frantic with fear, forced their way, and, pursued by nothing but their own terrified imaginations, they arrived at Brussels, proclaiming the dreadful news that the battle was lost, and the French advancing! The fearful tidings extended from thence even into Holland; and thus, in consequence of the cowardice of some Belgians and baggage-men, the last and most dreadful alarm of Sunday night was spread over the whole country.

The road, the whole way through the forest of Soignies, was marked with vestiges of the dreadful scenes which had recently taken place upon it. Bones of unburied horses, and pieces of broken carts and harness were scattered about. At every step we met with the remains of some tattered clothes, which had once been a soldier's. Shoes, belts, and scabbards, infantry caps battered to pieces, broken feathers and Highland bonnets covered with mud, were strewn along the road-side, or thrown among the trees. These mournful relics had belonged to the wounded who had attempted to crawl from the fatal field, and who, unable to proceed farther, had laid down and died upon the ground now marked by their graves—if holes dug by the way-side and hardly covered with earth deserved that name. The bodies of the wounded who died in the waggons on the way to Brussels had also been thrown out, and hastily interred.

Thus the road between Waterloo and Brussels was one long uninterrupted charnel-house : the smell, the whole way through the forest, was extremely offensive, and in some places scarcely bearable.   Deep stagnant pools of red putrid water, mingled with mortal remains, betrayed the spot where the bodies of men and horses had mingled together in death. We passed a large cross on the left side of the road, which had been erected in ancient times to mark the place where *one* human being had been murdered.   How many had now sunk around it in agony, and breathed, unnoticed and un- pitied, their dying groans!   It was surrounded by many a fresh-made, melancholy mound, which had served for the soldier's humble grave ; but no monument points out to future times the bloody spot where they expired; no cross stands to implore from the passenger the tribute of a tear, or call forth a pious prayer for the repose of the departed spirits who here perished for their country !

The melancholy vestiges of death and destruction became more frequent, the pools of putrid water more deep, and the smell more offensive, as we approached Waterloo, which is situated at the distance of about three leagues, or scarcely nine miles, from Brussels.   Before we left the forest, the Church of Waterloo appeared in view, at the end of the avenue of trees.   It is a singular building, much in the form of a Chinese temple, and built of red brick.   On leaving the wood, we passed the trampled and deep-marked bivouac, where the heavy baggage-waggons, tilted carts, and tumbrils had been stationed during the battle, and from which they had taken flight with such precipitation.

Even here cannon-balls had lodged in the trees, but had

passed over the roofs of the cottages. We entered the village which has given its name to the most glorious battle ever recorded in the annals of history. It was the Head-quarters of the British army on the nights preceding and following the battle. It was here the dispositions 'for the action were made on Saturday afternoon. It was here on Monday morning the dispatches were written, which perhaps contain the most brief and unassuming account a conqueror ever penned, of the most glorious victory that a conqueror ever won.* Waterloo consists of a sort of long, irregular street of whitewashed cottages, through which the road runs. Some of them are detached, and some built in rows. A small house, with a neat, little, square flower-garden before it, on the right hand, was pointed out to us as the quarters of Lord Uxbridge, and the place where he remained after the amputation of his leg, until well enough to bear removal. His name, and those of "His Grace the Duke of Wellington," "His Royal Highness the Prince of Orange," and other pompous titles, were written on the doors of these little thatched cottages. We also read the lamented names of Sir Thomas Picton, Sir Alexander Gordon, Sir William de Lancey, and Sir William Ponsonby, who had slept there the night before the battle, and many others who now sleep in the bed of honour. Volumes of sermons and homilies upon the instability of human life could not have spoken such affecting and convincing eloquence to our hearts as the sight of these names, thus traced in chalk, which had been more durable than the lives of these gallant men.

After leaving Waterloo, the ground rises: the wood,

* Cæsar's celebrated *bulletin*, "Veni, vidi, vici," was more concise, but not quite so unassuming.

which had opened, again surrounded us, though in a more straggling and irregular manner—and it was not till we arrived at the little village of Mont St. Jean, more than a mile beyond Waterloo, that we finally quitted the shade of the forest, and entered upon the open field where the battle had been fought. During the whole of the action the rear of the left wing of our army rested upon this little village, from which the French named the battle. We gazed with particular interest at a farm-house, at the farthest extremity of the village nearest the field, on the left side of the road,— with its walls and gates and roofs still bearing the vestiges of the cannon-balls that had pierced them. Every part of this house and offices was filled with wounded British officers; and here our friend Major L. was conveyed in excruciating agony, upon an old blanket, supported by the bayonets of four of his soldiers.

On the right we saw at some distance the church of Braine la Leude, which was in the rear of the extremity of the right wing of our army. From the top of the steeple of this church the battle might have been seen more distinctly than from any other place, if any one had possessed coolness and hardihood sufficient to have stood the calm spectator of such a scene; and if some cannot-ball had not stopped his observations by carrying off his head.

Alighting from the carriage, which we sent back to the barrière of Mont St. Jean, we walked past the place where the beaten down corn, and the whole appearance of the ground, would alone have been sufficient to have indicated that it had been the bivouac of the British army on the tempestuous night before the battle, when, after marching and fighting all day beneath a burning sun, they lay all night in this swampy piece of ground, under torrents of rain. We rapidly hurried on, until our progress was arrested by a long line of immense fresh-made graves. We suddenly stopped —we stood rooted to the spot—we gazed around us in silence; for the emotions that at this moment swelled our hearts were too deep for utterance—we felt that we stood on the field of battle!

"And these, then, are the graves of the brave!" at length mournfully exclaimed one of the party, after a silence of some minutes, hastily wiping away some "natural tears." "Look how they extend all along in front of this broken, beaten-down hedge—what tremendous slaughter!" "This is, or rather was," said an officer who was our conductor, "the hedge of La Haye Sainte;* the ground in front of it, and the narrow lane that runs behind it, were occupied by Sir Thomas Picton's division, which formed the left wing of the army; and it was in leading forward his men to a glorious and successful charge against a furious attack made by an immense force of the enemy, that this gallant and lamented officer fell. He was shot through the head, and died instantly, without uttering a word or a groan!" We gazed at the opposite height, or rather bank, upon which the French army was posted. We thought of the feelings with which our gallant soldiers must have viewed it, before the action commenced, when it was covered with the innumerable legions of France, ranged in arms against them. The solemn and portentous stillness which precedes the bursting of the tempest, is nothing to the awful sublimity of a moment such

* La Haye Sainte (the holy hedge). It gives its name to the farm-house of La Haye Sainte. I could not hear from any of the country people why it was distinguished by the epithet "Sainte." They did not seem to have any tradition respecting it.

as this. The threatening columns of that immense army, which their valour had destroyed and scattered, were then ready to pour down upon them. The cannon taken in the action, which now stood in the field before us under the guard of a single British soldier, were then turned against them.

The field-pieces taken by the Prussians in the pursuit were not here. But 130 pieces of cannon belonging to the British, and taken by them on the field of battle, still remained here. We went to examine them; they were beautiful pieces of ordnance, inscribed with very whimsical names, and some of them with the revolutionary words of Liberté, Egalité, Fraternité! Our own artillery, which was admirably served, had been principally placed in two lines upon the ridge of the gentle slope on which our army was stationed. About four o'clock in the afternoon the first line of guns advanced, and the second took the place which the first had before occupied; it was also placed upon every little eminence over the field, and it did great execution amongst the enemy's ranks.*

* An order had been issued not to fire at the enemy's field-pieces, but at the troops. However, during the latter part of the action, a young officer of artillery, out of patience with the destruction caused among his men, and particularly with the loss of Captain Bolton, his friend and brother officer, from the fire of some guns opposite, levelled his cannon at them, and had the satisfaction to see the French artillerymen, and officers who commanded them, fall in their turn. At that moment he was accosted suddenly by the Duke of Wellington, whom he had no idea was near— "What are you firing at there?" The artillery officer confessed what he was about. "Keep a good look out to your left," said the Duke, "you will see a large body of the enemy advancing just now—fire at them." They soon perceived a tremendous number of the Imperial Guards, the *élite* of the army, advancing with great order and steadiness to attack the British. The moment they appeared in view, the officer to whom the Duke had spoken, directed against them such a tremendous and effective fire, that they were mowed down by ranks. This gallant young officer had volunteered his services, and was one of the brigade attached to the second division of our army.

The ground occupied by Sir Thomas Picton's division, on the left of the road from Brussels, is lower than any other part of the British position. It is divided from the more elevated ridge where the French were posted by a very gentle declivity. To the right the ground rises, and the hollow irregularly increases, until at Château Hougoumont it becomes a sort of small dell or ravine, and the banks are both high and steep. But the ground occupied by the French is uniformly higher, and decidedly a stronger position than ours.

Nothing struck me with more surprise than the confined space in which this tremendous battle had been fought; and this, perhaps, in some measure contributed to its sanguinary result. The space which divided the two armies from the farm-house of La Haye Sainte, which was occupied by our troops, to La Belle Alliance, which was occupied by theirs, would, I think, scarcely measure three furlongs. Not more than half a mile could have intervened between the main body of the French and English armies; and from the extremity of the right to that of the left wing of our army, I should suppose to be little more than a mile.

The hedge along which Sir Thomas Picton's division was stationed, and through which the Scots Greys, with the Royals and the Inniskillens, headed by Lord Uxbridge, made their glorious and decisive charge at the close of the action, is almost the only one in the field of battle. The ground is occasionally divided by some shallow ditches, and in one place there is a sort of low mud dyke, which was very much broken and beaten down. This was not on the ground our troops occupied, but rather below the French position ; and excepting this, the whole field of battle is unenclosed. The

K

ground is, however, very uneven and broken, and the soil a strong clay. It belongs to different farmers, and bore crops of different kinds of corn; but it is entirely arable land, and, excepting a very small piece on the French side, none of it was in grass.

Against the left wing of our army the attacks of the French were furious and incessant. Buonaparte had stationed opposite to it the chief body of his Corps de Réserve, and fresh columns of troops continually poured down, without being able to make the smallest impression upon the firm and impenetrable squares which the British regiments formed to receive them. It was Buonaparte's object to turn the left wing of our army, and cut it off from the Prussians, with whom a communication was maintained through Ohain, and who were known (at least by the commanders of the British army) to be advancing.* The Duke expected them to have joined before one o'clock, but it was seven before they made their appearance.

On the top of the ridge in front of the British position, on the left of the road, we traced a long line of tremendous graves, or rather pits, into which hundreds of dead had been thrown as they had fallen in their ranks, without yielding an inch of ground. The effluvia which arose from them, even beneath the open canopy of heaven, was horrible; and the pure west wind of summer, as it passed us, seemed pestiferous, so deadly was the smell that in many places pervaded the field. The fresh-turned clay which covered those pits

---

* It is, however, a remarkable fact, and does additional honour to the resolute, invincible constancy of British soldiers, that nearly all the officers, and the whole of the privates of the British army, were ignorant that there was any expectation of the arrival of the Prussians. Indeed, many of them never knew till after the battle was over that they had joined.

betrayed how recent had been their formation. From one of them the scanty clods of earth which had covered it had in one place fallen, and the skeleton of a human face was visible. I turned from the spot in indescribable horror, and with a sensation of deadly faintness which I could scarcely overcome.

On the opposite side of the road we scrambled up a perpendicular bank, through which the road had evidently been cut. It was upon this eminence that the Duke of Wellington stood, beneath the memorable tree, from the commencement of the action, surrounded by his staff. It was here, we were told, that in the most critical part of it he rallied the different regiments, and led them on again in person to renew the shock of battle. Here we stood some time to survey the field.

Immediately before us, nearly in the hollow, was the farm-house of La Haye Sainte, surrounded by a quadrangular wall, full of holes for musketry. At the commencement of the action it was occupied by the British, and it formed the most advanced post of the left centre of our army. It was gallantly and successfully defended by a detachment of the light battalion of the German Legion, until nearly the close of the day, when their ammunition was exhausted; it was impossible to send them a supply, as all communication with them was cut off by the enemy, who at length succeeded in carrying it, after a most obstinate resistance; but its brave defenders only resigned its possession with their lives.

On the opposite side of the road, a little behind La Haye Sainte, and immediately below the ground occupied by Sir Thomas Picton's division, is a quarry which was surrounded by British artillery at the commencement of the battle. Towards the close of the action it was filled with the wounded, who had taken refuge in it as a shelter from the shot and shells, and from the charge of the cavalry—when, horrible to relate! a body of French Cuirassiers were completely overthrown ·into this quarry by a furious charge of the British, and horses and riders were rolled in death upon these unfortunate sufferers. The ghastly spectacle which it exhibited next morning was described to me by an eye-witness of this scene of horror. On the left, in the hollow between the two armies, we saw the hamlet of Ter la Haye, which was occupied by British troops;—its possession was never disputed by the enemy, although it was close advanced upon their position. Beyond it, still farther to the left, were the woods of Frischermont, and the road to Wavre, from which the Prussians issued through a narrow defile, and advanced to attack the right flank of the French.

These woods bounded the prospect on that side. On the right stood the ruins of Château Hougoumont (or Château Goumont, as the country-people called it), concealed from view by a small wood which crowns the hill. It formed the most advanced post of the right centre of our army, and it was defended to the last with efforts of successful valour, almost more than human, against the overpowering numbers and furious attacks of the enemy. The battle commenced here about eleven o'clock. The French, suddenly uncovering a masked battery, opened a tremendous fire upon this part of our position, and advanced to the attack with astonishing impetuosity, led on, it is said, by Jerome Buonaparte in person, while Napoleon viewed it from his station near the Observatory on the opposite height. They were completely repulsed by the bravery of General Byng's brigade of Guards, but they succeeded in carrying the wood, which was occupied by the Belgic troops. The French, however.

after a dreadful struggle, were driven out of the wood again by the Coldstreams and the third regiment of Guards, and never afterwards were able to regain possession of it. The Black Brunswickers behaved most gallantly. In retrieving the consequences of the misconduct of the Belgic troops, and in defending the Château and the garden, the British Guards performed prodigies of valour, though they suffered most severely. Lieutenant-General Cooke, Major-General Byng, Lord Saltoun, the lamented Colonel Miller, who died as he had lived—a brave and honourable soldier; Captain Adair, Captains Evelyn and Ellis; Colonels Askew, Dashwood, and D'Oyley, with many others, particularly distinguished themselves by their steady gallantry and personal valour. The house was consumed by fire, and numbers of the wounded perished in the flames; yet the British maintained possession of it to the last, in spite of the incessant and desperate attacks of the enemy, who directed against it a furious fire of shot and shells, under cover of which large bodies of troops advanced continually to the assault, and were driven back again and again with tremendous slaughter. Without the possession of this important post the right flank of our army could not be attacked; it formed what is called the key of the position; from its elevation it commanded the whole of the ground occupied by our army, and had it been lost, the victory to the French would scarcely have been doubtful.

Opposite, but divided from it by a deep hollow, were the heights occupied by the French, upon which, at some distance, and secure from the storm of war, stands the Observatory, where Buonaparte stationed himself at the beginning of the action, and whence he issued his orders, and commanded column after column to advance to the charge, and rush upon destruction. His " invincible" legions, his invulnerable Cuirassiers, in vain assaulted the position of the British with the most furious and undaunted resolution.   In vain the vast tide of battle rolled on—like the rocks of their native land, they repelled its rage.—Squares of infantry received the onset of the French columns; directed against them a steady and uninterrupted fire of musketry, and stood firm and unshaken beneath the most tremendous showers of shot and shell.   Every vacancy caused by death was instantly filled up: the enemy vainly sought for an opening through which they might penetrate the impenetrable phalanx; and when at last they receded from the ineffectual attack, the British cavalry rushed forward to the charge, and, notwithstanding their superiority of numbers, drove them back with immense slaughter.   But I am relating the history of the battle, forgetful that I am only describing the field.

From the spot where we now stood I cast my eyes on every side, and saw nothing but the dreadful and recent traces of death and devastation.   The rich harvests of standing corn,* which had covered the scene of action we were contemplating, had been beaten into the earth, and the withered and broken stalks dried in the sun, now presented the appearance of stubble, though blacker and far more bare than any stubble land.

In many places the excavations made by the shells had thrown up the earth all around them; the marks of horses' hoofs, that had plunged ankle deep in clay, were hardened

---

* In this part of Belgium, the wheat had this year grown to full five feet in height, and rye upwards of six feet: great quantities of the latter are grown, for it answers to the liberal definition of oats by Dr. Johnson, and is the food of men in England, and of horses in Flanders; nay, it is actually baked into bread for their use, and regularly given them at the inns where they stop to bait.   Several soldiers of the Highland regiments who had got into a field of this gigantic rye on the 16th, were shot without even being able to see their enemy.

in the sun; and the feet of men, deeply stamped into the ground, left traces where many a deadly struggle had been. The ground was ploughed up in several places with the charge of the cavalry, and the whole field was literally covered with soldiers' caps, shoes, gloves, belts, and scabbards; broken feathers battered into the mud, remnants of tattered scarlet or blue cloth, bits of fur and leather, black stocks and havresacs, belonging to the French soldiers, buckles, packs of cards, books, and innumerable papers of every description. I picked up a volume of Candide; a few sheets of sentimental love-letters, evidently belonging to some French novel; and many other pages of the same publication were flying over the field in much too muddy a state to be touched. One German Testament, not quite so dirty as many that were lying about, I carried with me nearly the whole day; printed French military returns, muster rolls, love-letters, and washing bills; illegible songs, scattered sheets of military music, epistles without number in praise of " l'Empereur, le Grand Napoléon," and filled with the most confident anticipations of victory under his command, were strewed over the field which had been the scene of his defeat. The quantities of letters and of blank sheets of dirty writing paper were so great that they literally whitened the surface of the earth.

The road to Genappe, descending from the front of the British position, where we were now standing, passes the farm-house of La Haye Sainte, and ascends the opposite height, on the summit of which stands La Belle Alliance, which was occupied by the French. We walked down the hill to La Haye Sainte—its walls and slated roofs were shattered and pierced through in every direction with cannon shot. We could not get admittance into it, for it was completely deserted by its inhabitants. Three wounded officer

of the 42nd and 92nd Regiments were standing here to
survey the scene: they had all of them been wounded in the
battle of the 16th.   One of them had lost an arm, another
was on crutches, and the third seemed to be very ill.   Their
carriage waited for them, as they were unable to walk.
After some conversation with them, we proceeded up the hill
to the hamlet of La Belle Alliance.   The principal house on
the left side of the road was pierced through and through
with cannon balls, and the offices behind it were a heap of
dust from the fire of the British artillery.   Notwithstanding
the ruinous state of the house, it was filled with inhabitants.
Its broken walls, " its looped and windowed wretchedness,"
might indeed defend them sufficiently " well from seasons
such as these," when the soft breezes and the bright beams
of summer played around it—but against " the pelting of the
storm," it would afford them but a sorry shelter.   It was immediately to be repaired ; but I rejoiced that it yet remained
in its dilapidated state.

The house was filled with vestiges of the battle. Cuirasses,
helmets, swords, bayonets, feathers, brass eagles, and crosses
of the Legion of Honour, were to be purchased here.   The
house consisted of three rooms, two in front, and a very
small one behind.   On the opposite side of the road is a
little cottage, forming part of the hamlet of La Belle
Alliance; and at a short distance, by the way side, is
another low-roofed cottage, which was pointed out to us as
the place where Buonaparte breakfasted on the morning of
the battle.   Farther along this road, but not in sight, was
the village of Planchenoit, which was the head-quarters of
the French on the night of the 17th.*

* Buonaparte slept at the farm of Caillou, near Planchenoit.

We crossed the field from this place to Château Hougoumont, descending to the bottom of the hill, and again ascending the opposite side. Part of our way lay through clover; but I observed that the corn on the French position was not nearly so much beaten down as on the English, which might naturally be expected, as they attacked us incessantly, and we acted on the defensive, until that last, general, and decisive charge of our whole army was made, before which theirs fled in confusion. In some places patches of corn nearly as high as myself was standing. Among them I discovered many a forgotten grave, strewed round with melancholy remnants of military attire. While I loitered behind the rest of the party, searching among the corn for some relics worthy of preservation, I beheld a human hand, almost reduced to a skeleton, outstretched above the ground, as if it had raised itself from the grave. My blood ran cold with horror, and for some moments I stood rooted to the spot, unable to take my eyes from this dreadful object, or to move away: as soon as I recovered myself, I hastened after my companions, who were far before me, and overtook them just as they entered the wood of Hougoumont. Never shall I forget the dreadful scene of death and destruction which it presented. The broken branches were strewed around, the green beech leaves fallen before their time, and stripped by the storm of war, not by the storm of Nature, were scattered over the surface of the ground, emblematical of the fate of the thousands who had fallen on the same spot in the summer of their days. The return of spring will dress the wood of Hougoumont once more in vernal beauty, and succeeding years will see it flourish:

"But when shall spring visit the mouldering urn,
Oh! when shall it dawn on the night of the grave!"

The trunks of the trees had been pierced in every direction with cannon-balls. In some of them I counted the holes, where upwards of thirty had lodged:* yet they still lived, they still bore their verdant foliage, and the birds still sang amidst their boughs. Beneath their shade the hare-bell and violet were waving their slender heads; and the wild raspberry at their roots was ripening its fruit. I gathered some of it with the bitter reflection, that amidst the destruction of human life these worthless weeds and flowers had escaped uninjured.

Melancholy were the vestiges of death that continually met our eyes. The carnage here had indeed been dreadful. Amongst the long grass lay remains of broken arms, shreds of gold lace, torn epaulets, and pieces of cartridge boxes; and upon the tangled branches of the brambles fluttered many a tattered remnant of a soldier's coat. At the outskirts of the wood, and around the ruined walls of the Château, huge piles of human ashes were heaped up, some of which were still smoking. The countrymen told us, that so great were the numbers of the slain, that it was impossible entirely to consume them. Pits had been dug, into which they had been thrown, but they were obliged to be raised far above the surface of the ground. These dreadful heaps were covered with piles of wood, which were set on fire, so that underneath the ashes lay numbers of human bodies unconsumed.

The Château itself, the beautiful seat of a Belgic gentle-

* These memorable beech-trees, pierced through and through with balls, have been since all cut down by the owner of Château Hougoumont!!!

man, had been set on fire by the explosion of shells during the action, which had completed the destruction occasioned by a most furious cannonade. Its broken walls and falling roof presented a most melancholy spectacle: not melancholy merely from its being a pile of ruins, but from the vestiges it presented of that tremendous and recent warfare by which those ruins had been caused. Its huge blackened beams had fallen in every direction upon the crumbling heaps of stone and plaster, which were intermixed with broken pieces of the marble flags, the carved cornices, and the gilded mirrors, that once ornamented it.

We went into the garden, which had sustained comparatively little injury, while every thing around it was laid waste. Its gay parterres and summer flowers made it look like an island in the desert. A berçeau, or covered walk, ran round it, shaded with creeping plants, amongst which honey-suckles and jessamines were intermixed, en treillage. The trees were loaded with fruit ; the myrtles and fig-trees were flourishing in luxuriance, and the scarlet geraniums, July flowers, and orange-trees, were in full blow. My native country can boast of no such beauty as bloomed at Château Hougoumont : its rugged clime produces no fruitful fig-trees, no flowers rich in the fragrance of orange blossom :— but it is the land of heroes !

> " Man is the nobler growth our realms supply,
> And souls are ripened in our northern sky."

I saw the pure and polished leaves of the laurel shining in the sun, and I could not restrain my tears at the thought that the laurels, the everlasting laurels which England had won upon this spot, were steeped in the heart-blood of thousands of her brave, her lamented sons. But if not immortal in their lives, they will be so in their fame: their laurels will never wither ; and no British heart, henceforward, will ever visit this hallowed spot without paying a tribute of veneration and regret to those gallant spirits who here fought and fell for their country.

At the garden gate I found the holster of a British officer, entire, but deluged with blood. In the inside was the maker's name—Beazley and Hetse, No. 4, Parliament-street. All around were strewed torn epaulets, broken scabbards, and sabretashes stained and stiffened with blood—proofs how dreadfully the battle had raged. The garden and courts were lined during the engagement with Nassau troops, as sharpshooters, who did great execution.

A poor countryman, with his wife and children, inhabited a miserable shed amongst these deserted ruins. This unfortunate family had only fled from the spot on the morning of the battle. Their little dwelling had been burnt, and all their property had perished in the flames. They had scarcely clothes to cover them, and were destitute of everything. Yet the poor woman, as she told me the story of their distresses, and wept over the baby that she clasped to her breast, blessed heaven that she had preserved her children. She seemed most grateful for a little assistance, took me into her miserable habitation, and gave me the broken sword of a British officer of infantry (most probably of the Guards), which was the only thing she had left ; and which, with some other relics before collected, I preserved as carefully as if they had been the most valuable treasures.

It is a remarkable circumstance that amidst this scene of destruction, and surrounded on all sides by the shattered walls and smoking piles of "this ruined and roofless abode," the little chapel belonging to the Château stood uninjured. Its preservation appeared to these simple peasants an unquestionable miracle; and we felt more inclined to respect than to wonder at the superstitious veneration with which they regarded it. No shot nor shell had penetrated its consecrated walls ; no sacrilegious hand had dared to violate its humble altar, which was still adorned with its ancient ornaments and its customary care. A type of that blessed religion to which it was consecrated, it stood alone, unchanged, amidst the wreck of earthly greatness—as if to speak to our hearts, amidst the horrors of the tomb, the promises of immortality ; and to recal our thoughts from the crimes and sorrows of earth to the hopes and happiness of heaven. The voice of the Divinity himself within his holy temple seemed to tell us, that those whom we lamented here, and who, in the discharge of their last and noblest duty to their country, had met on the field of honour "the death that best becomes the brave,"—should receive in another and a better world their great reward ! Blackened piles of human ashes surrounded us ; but I felt that though "the dust returns to the earth, the spirit returns unto Him that gave it."

The countryman led me to one of these piles within the gates of the court belonging to the Château, where, he said, the bodies of three hundred of the British Guardsmen who had so gallantly defended it, had been burnt as they had been found, heaped in death.* I took some of the ashes and wrapped them up in one of the many sheets of paper that were strewed around me ; perhaps those heaps that then blackened the surface of this scene of desolation are already

---

* In other pits the corpses of the French had also been burned. About eight thousand of the French army fell in the attack of Hougoumont.

scattered by the winds of winter, and mingled unnoticed
with the dust of the field; perhaps the few sacred ashes
which I then gathered at Château Hougoumont are all that
is now to be found upon earth of the thousands who fell
upon this fatal field!

. It was not without regret that we left this ever-memorable spot, surrounded as it was by horrors that shocked
the mind, and vestiges that were revolting to the senses.
Still we lingered around it, till at length, after gazing for
the last time at its ruined archways and desolated courts, we
struck into the wood, and lost sight for ever of the Château
Hougoumont. The road to Nivelles, which strikes off to the
right from the highroad to Genappe at the village of Mont
St. Jean, passes the Château on the other side. The right
wing of the British army crossed this road, and in the deep
ditches on each side of it we were told that human remains
still lay uninterred. Some of the party returned to Mont
St. Jean by this road, which is considerably nearer; but my
brother, my sister, and myself, once more crossed the field
in order to pay another visit to La Belle Alliance.

I could not be persuaded to go to see the skeleton of a calf
which had been burnt in one of the outhouses of Hougoumont, and over which one of the ladies of our party uttered
the most pathetic lamentations. It seemed to fill her mind
with more concern than anything else. At another time I
might have been sorry for the calf; but when I remembered
how many poor wounded men had been burnt alive in these
ruins, it was impossible to bestow a single thought upon its
fate. Finding that her sensibility obtained no sympathy
from me, the lady turned to my sister, and began to bewail
the calf anew, till at last, wearied out with such folly, " out of

her grief and her impatience," she exclaimed, " that she did not care if all the calves in the world had been burnt, compared to one of the brave men who had perished here."

As we passed again through the wood of Hougoumont, I gathered some seeds of the wild broom, with the intention of planting them at H. Park, and with the hope that I should one day see the broom of Hougoumont blooming on the banks of the Tweed. In leaving the wood I was struck with the sight of the scarlet poppy flaunting in full bloom upon some new-made graves, as if in mockery of the dead. In many parts of the field these flowers were growing in profusion: they had probably been protected from injury by the tall and thick corn amongst which they grew, and their slender roots had adhered to the clods of clay which had been carelessly thrown upon the graves. From one of these graves I gathered the little wild blue flower known by the sentimental name of " Forget me not!" which to a romantic imagination might have furnished a fruitful subject for poetic reverie or pensive reflection.

While my sister was taking a view of the field of battle, and my brother was overlooking and guarding her, I entered the cottage of " La Belle Alliance," and began to talk to Baptiste la Coste, Buonaparte's guide, whom I found there. He is a sturdy, honest-looking countryman, and gave an interesting account of Buonaparte's behaviour during the battle. He said that he issued his orders with great vehemence, and even impatience: he took snuff incessantly, but in a hurried manner, and apparently from habit, and without being conscious that he was doing so: he talked a great deal, and very rapidly—his manner of speaking was abrupt, quick, and hurried: he was extremely nervous and agitated at times, though his anticipations of victory were most confident. He frequently expressed his astonishment, rather angrily, that the British held out so long—at the same time he could not repress his admiration of their gallantry, and often broke out into exclamations of amazement and approbation of their courage and conduct. He particularly admired the Scotch Greys—" Voilà ces chevaux gris—ah ! ce sont beaux cavaliers—très beaux;" and then he said they would all be cut to pieces. He said—" These English certainly fight well, but they must soon give way;" and he asked Soult, who was near him, " if he did not think so?" Soult replied, " He was afraid not." " And why?" said Napoleon, turning round to him quickly. " Because," said Soult, " I believe they will first be cut to pieces." Soult's opinion of the British army, which was founded on experience, coincided with that of the Duke of Wellington. " It will take a great many hours to cut them in pieces," said the Duke, in answer to something that was said to him during the action; " and I know they will never give way."

Buonaparte, however, who knew less of them, and whose head always ran upon the idea of the English flying to their ships, had never dreamt that with a force so inferior they would think of giving him battle, but imagined that they would continue their retreat during the night, and that he should have to pursue them. It is said that he expressed great satisfaction when the morning broke and he saw them still there; and that he exclaimed, " Ah ! pour le coup—je les tiens donc—ces Anglais !"

Before the engagement began he harangued the army, promising them the plunder of Brussels and Ghent. Once, towards the close of the battle, he addressed himself to the

Imperial Guard, leading them on to the brink of the hill, and telling them " that was the road to Brussels." Regardless of the waste of human life, he incessantly ordered his battalions to advance—to bear down upon the enemy—to carry every thing before them. He inflamed their ardour by the remembrance of past, as well as the prospect of present victory, and the promise of future reward: but he never led them on to battle himself—he never once braved the shock of British arms. It is not true as has been reported, that he was ever near Lord Uxbridge, or in any danger of being taken prisoner by the English. Indeed, he exposed himself to very little personal risk—a proof of which is, that not one of those who attended him the whole day was wounded.

La Coste said, that at first, when he was told that the Prussians were advancing, he obstinately and angrily refused to believe it, declaring it was the French corps under Marshal Grouchy.* He then commanded this news to be spread amongst the army, and ordered Marshal Ney, at the head of two columns, each composed of four battalions of the old Imperial Guard, and seconded by all the available force of the French army, both cavalry and infantry, to charge, and to penetrate to the centre of the British position. He stood to witness the desperate struggle which ensued, and the final and complete overthrow of the *élite* of his gallant army, or immensely preponderating force, by a handful of determined

* That Buonaparte pretended to believe those troops to be French, although he must have known the contrary, is unquestionably true. Marshal Ney, in his account of the battle, states that he received a message from the emperor, brought by General Labedoyère, to inform him " that the French corps under Marshal Grouchy had arrived in the field, and attacked the left wing of the British and Prussians united. General Labedoyère rode along the lines, spreading this intelligence through the whole army."—Vide *Marshal Ney's Letter.* [*See* Appendix, O.]

British troops ; but when he perceived his " invincible legions" give way, and retreat in confusion before the grand simultaneous charge of the British army, which immediately ensued, led by the Duke of Wellington in person, who was amongst the foremost in the onset, he turned pale, his perturbation became extreme, and exclaiming, " All is lost—let us save ourselves" (Tout est perdu ; or, Sauve qui peut !), or words to that effect; he put spurs to his horse, and galloped from the field. La Coste expressly said, that he was among the first of the officers to set the example of flight.*   His own old Imperial Guard still remained—disputed every foot of ground—fought desperately to the last, and at length, overpowered by numbers, fell gloriously—as their leader should have fallen.

But he !—not even despair could prompt him to one noble thought, or rouse him to one deed of desperate valour. He fled —as at Egypt, at Moscow, and at Leipsic he had fled—while his faithful veterans were still fighting with enthusiastic gallantry, and shedding the last drop of their blood in his cause !

Was this the conduct of a hero? Was this the conduct of a general? Was this the conduct of a great mind ? No! He had set his " life upon a cast, and he should have stood the hazard of the die." And for what did he abandon his army, and basely fly in the hour of danger? That he might be humiliated, pursued, and taken—that he might become a suppliant to that hated enemy whose ruin he had pursued with implacable hostility, and be indebted to their faith and generosity for life and safety—that he might live to hear his

---

* This statement too is confirmed by Marshal Ney, who said, " that Buonaparte had entirely disappeared before the end of the battle." Let it be remembered that Ney's letter was written exactly a week after the battle, while Napoleon was still emperor, and still in Paris, and. if his statement was not true, a thousand witnesses could have contradicted it.

name execrated, and linger out a few years of miserable existence in exile, obscurity, and degradation.

It has been said by his advocates and admirers, that he was not only a great man, but the greatest man who ever lived—and that his only fault was ambition. Yes! Napoleon Buonaparte had, indeed, ambition; but it was selfish ambition; it was for power, not for glory; for unbounded empire and unlimited dominion, not for the welfare of his subjects and the prosperity of his country. He used the talents, the opportunities, and the power, with which he was gifted, and such as perhaps no mortal ever before enjoyed, not to save, but to destroy, not to bless, but to desolate, the world.

The conduct of the leaders of the contending armies was as opposite as the cause for which they fought. While Napoleon kept aloof from the action, Lord Wellington exposed himself to the hottest fire, threw himself into the thickest of the fight, and braved every danger of the battle. He issued every order, he directed every movement, he seemed to be everywhere present, he encouraged his troops, he rallied his regiments, he led them on against the tremendous forces of the enemy, charged at their head, and defeated their most formidable attacks. No private soldier in his army was exposed to half the personal danger that he encountered.* All who surrounded him fell by his side, wounded and dying. All his personal staff, with scarcely an exception, were either killed or wounded. In the battle's most terrible moment, and most hopeless crisis, when our gallant army, weakened by immense losses, and by more than seven hours of unequal combat, were scarcely able to stand against the overwhelm-

* The Duke himself reverentially said afterwards, "The finger of God was upon me."

ing number of fresh troops which the enemy poured down against them; when the recreant Belgians fled, when every British soldier was in action, when reinforcements were asked for in vain; when no reserve remained, and no prospect of succour from our allies appeared, Lord Wellington, exposed to the hottest fire, calmly rode along the lines of his diminished army, animating and encouraging the men; directed fresh arrangements of his remaining forces; rallied in the fight, the wavering Brunswickers, cheered on, and headed the brave British Brigades,* and finally, having repulsed the last tremendous attack of the enemy,—with the memorable words, "Up guards! and at them!" led on the remnant of his gallant army to the most glorious victory a general ever won.†

Nor was the conduct of the two generals on this day more opposite than that of the armies which they commanded, and the motives by which they were actuated. The French fought to obtain plunder and aggrandisement—the British to fulfil their duty to their country. Well did their generals know this essential difference! Buonaparte held out to his troops the spoils of Belgium and Holland. When he wished to animate them to the greatest exertions, he led them forward and told them, "That was the road to Brussels!" Lord Wellington, in the most critical moment of the battle, held another language. "We must not be beaten," he said to his soldiers; "what will they say of us in England!" After the battle their conduct was equally different. The French had murdered numbers of their prisoners, and those whose

---

* It was near seven o'clock when this circumstance happened. The Prussians had not appeared. The regiments which he led to the charge were the 71st, the 52nd, and the 95th. He also repeatedly rallied the Belgic regiments, and sometimes vainly exerted himself to make them face the enemy.   † [See Appendix, D.]

lives they spared, they robbed, insulted, and treated with the utmost cruelty, shutting them up without food, without dressing their wounds, and subjecting them to every hardship and privation. The British, on the contrary, though irritated by the knowledge of these barbarities, protected the wounded French from the rage of the Prussians, who would have gladly revenged the cruelties with which they had been treated by them. Our wounded soldiers, who were able to move, employed themselves in assisting their suffering enemies, binding up their wounds, and giving them food and water—but the brave are always merciful.

A countryman, who belonged either to La Belle Alliance, or to some of the neighbouring cottages, told me, that when he came here early on the morning after the battle, the house was surrounded with the wounded and dying of the French army, many of whom implored him, for God's sake, to put an end to their sufferings.

But the agonising scenes which had so recently taken place here, and the images of horror which every object in and around La Belle Alliance was irresistibly calculated to suggest to the mind, were almost too dreadful for reflection. More pleasing was the remembrance, that it was here Napoleon Buonaparte stood when he prematurely dispatched a courier to Paris with the false news that he had won the day; and that it was here the Duke of Wellington and Marshal Blucher accidently met, a few hours after, in the very moment of victory, when Buonaparte was flying before their triumphant armies, himself the bearer of the news of his own defeat. [*See* Appendix, E.]

The interview between the Duke of Wellington and Marshal Blucher was short, but it will be for ever memorable in the annals of history. They did not enter the house, but re-

mained together a few minutes in earnest conversation. It
is well known that Blucher and the Prussians continued the
pursuit during the night. The remains of the British army
rested from their toils on the ground, surrounded by the
bleeding and dying French, on the very spot which they had
occupied the preceding night—and Lord Wellington returned to Waterloo.

" As he crossed again the fatal field, on which the silence
of death had now succeeded to the storm of battle, the
moon, breaking from dark clouds, shed an uncertain light
upon this wide scene of carnage, covered with mangled thousands of that gallant army whose heroic valour had won
for him the brightest wreath of victory, and left to future
times an imperishable monument of their country's fame.
He saw himself surrounded by the bloody corpses of his veteran soldiers, who had followed him through distant lands,
of his friends, his associates in arms, his companions through
many an eventful year of danger and of glory : in that awful
pause, which follows the mortal conflict of man with man,
emotions, unknown or stifled in the heat of battle, forced
their way—the feelings of the man triumphed over those of
the general, and in the very hour of victory Lord Wellington
burst into tears."*

* It was with a heart saddened by feelings which did him honour, that
the Duke of Wellington returned from the battle. The letters which he
wrote to the relations of the distinguished officers who had fallen, prove
how truly he felt what he sorrowfully said, that " there is nothing more
melancholy than a victory—except a defeat." I cannot resist inserting
the following simple and affecting extract from one of his letters, written
on the morning after the battle. " I cannot express to you," he writes,
" the regret and sorrow with which I look around me, and contemplate
the losses which I have sustained. They have quite broken me down.
The glory resulting from such actions, so dearly bought, is no consolation to me."

The extract in the text is taken " From Circumstantial Details Relative
to the Battle of Waterloo," which was written by the author to explain

The state of the wounded during this dreadful night may be conceived. Not even a drop of water was to be had on the field to relieve their thirst, and none was to be procured nearer than Waterloo. Late as it was, and exhausted as our officers must have been with the fatigue of such unremitting exertions, many of them mounted their horses, slung over their shoulders as many canteens as they could carry, galloped to Waterloo, a distance of more than two miles from almost every part of the field, filled them with water, and returned with it for the relief of the wounded men.

I did not leave a corner of La Belle Alliance unrummaged, but I cannot say that I saw anything particularly worthy of notice: I ate a bit of intolerably bad rye-cake, as sour as vinegar, and as black as the bread of Sparta, which nothing but the consideration of its having been in La Belle Alliance during the battle (which the woman assured me was the case) could have induced me to swallow:—but I need not stop to relate my own follies.

I bought from the people of the house the feather of a French officer, and a cuirass which had belonged to a French Cuirassier, who, they said, had died here the day after the battle. Loaded with my spoils, I traversed the whole extent of the field, thinking, as I toiled along beneath the burning sun, under the weight of the heavy cuirass, that the poor man to whom it had belonged, when he brought it into the field, in all the pride of martial ardour, and all the confidence of victory, little dreamed who would carry it off. If he had known that it was to be an English lady, he would have been more surprised than pleased.

" A Panoramic Sketch of the Field of Battle," by her sister, both of which were published by J. Booth, London, in August, 1815, for the benefit of the Waterloo Fund.

I did not stop till I got to the old tree now known by the name of Lord Wellington's tree,* near which he stood for a length of time during the battle, and beneath which I now sat myself down to rest. Its massy trunk and broken branches were pierced with a number of cannon-balls, but its foliage still afforded me a grateful shade from the rays of the sun.

It was between this part of the field and Hougoumont that the lamented Sir William Ponsonby gloriously fell in the prime of life and honour, after repeatedly leading the most gallant and successful charges against the enemy, in which he took upwards of 2000 prisoners and two French eagles. The particulars of his death are well known. In the heat of the action he was unfortunately separated from his brigade, his horse stuck fast in the deep wet clay of some newly-ploughed land, and he saw a large body of Polish Lancers bearing down against him. In this dreadful situation he awaited the inevitable fate that approached him with the composure of a hero: he calmly turned to his aide-de-camp, who was still by his side, and it is said that he was in the act of giving him a picture and a last message to his wife, when he was pierced at once with the pikes of seven of the Polish Lancers, and fell covered with wounds. England never lost a better soldier, nor society a brighter ornament. He was deservedly beloved by his friends and companions, adored by his family, and lamented and honoured by his country.

Numbers of country-people were employed in what might be called the gleanings of the harvest of spoil. The muskets, the swords, the helmets, the cuirasses—all the large and un-

* It is on the left of the road in going towards Waterloo, behind the farm-house of La Haye Sainte. But this tree, which ought to have been for ever sacred, has been CUT DOWN!!!

broken arms had been immediately carried off; and now the eagles that had emblazoned the caps of the French infantry, the fragments of broken swords, &c., were rarely to be found, though there was great abundance upon sale. But there was still plenty of rubbish to be picked up upon the field, for those who had a taste for it like me—though the greatest part of it was in a most horrible state.

It was astonishing with what dreadful haste the bodies of the dead had been pillaged. The work of plunder was carried on even during the battle ; and those hardened and abandoned wretches who follow the camp, like vultures, to prey upon the corpses of the dead, had the temerity to press forward beneath a heavy fire to rifle the pockets of the officers who fell of their watches and money. The most daring and atrocious of these marauders were women.*

The description I heard of the field the morning after the battle from those who had visited it, I cannot yet recal without horror. Horses were galloping about in every direction without their riders: some of them, bleeding with their

---

* Some soldiers' wives were, however, actuated by better motives, and, like the matrons of Hensberg, in times of old, seemed to think their best treasures were their husbands. Many of them rushed forward and carried their wounded husbands off the field at the hazard of their own lives. The wife of a sergeant in the 28th was severely wounded in two places by a shell, which struck her as she was carrying off her wounded husband. This anecdote was related to me by an eye-witness of the circumstance. The woman (respecting whom I inquired since my return to England) has, I understand, been allowed a pension from Chelsea Hospital. I heard of several similar instances of heroic conjugal affection; and I myself saw one poor woman, the wife of a private in the 27th, whose leg was dreadfully fractured by a musket-ball in rescuing her husband. When struck by the ball she fell to the ground with her husband, who was supposed to be mortally wounded, but she still refused to leave him, and they were removed together to the rear, and afterwards sent to Antwerp. The poor man survived the amputation of both his arms, and is still alive. The woman, who was then in a state of pregnancy, has, since her return to this country, given birth to a child, to which the Duke of York stood godfather.

wounds and frantic with pain, were tearing up the ground, and plunging over the bodies of the dead and the dying—and many of them were lying on the ground in the agonies of death.

Over the whole field the bodies of the innumerable dead, already stripped of every covering, were lying in heaps upon each other; the wounded in many instances beneath them. Some, faint and bleeding, were slowly attempting to make their way towards Brussels; others were crawling upon their hands and knees from this scene of misery; and many, unable to move, lay on the ground in agony.

For four days and nights some of these unfortunate men were exposed to the beams of the sun by day, and to the dews by night; for notwithstanding the most praiseworthy and indefatigable exertions, the last of the wounded were not removed from the field until the Thursday after the battle; and if we consider that there were at least 8000 British, besides the Belgic, Brunswick, and Prussian wounded soldiers, and an incalculable number of wounded French— we shall find cause for surprise and admiration, that they could be removed in so short a time. Their conveyance, too, was rendered extremely difficult, as well as inconceivably painful to the poor sufferers, by the dreadful and almost impassable state of the roads.

The Belgic peasantry showed the most active and attentive humanity to these poor wounded men. They brought them the best food they could procure; they gave them water to drink—they ministered to all their wants—complied with all their wishes—and treated them as if they had been their own children.

An officer, with whom we are well acquainted, went over the field on the morning of the battle, and examined the ghastly heaps of dead in search of the body of a near relation ; and after all the corpses were buried or burnt—in the same melancholy and fruitless search, many an English-woman, whom this day of glory had bereft of husband or son, wandered over this fatal field, wildly calling upon the names of those who were now no more. The very day before we visited it, the widow and the sister of a brave and lamented British officer had been here, harrowing up the souls of the beholders with their wild lamentations, vainly demanding where the remains of him they loved reposed, and accusing Heaven for denying them the consolation of weeping over his grave. I was myself, afterwards, a sorrowful witness of the dreadful effects of the unrestrained indulgence of this passionate and heart-breaking grief. In the instance to which I allude, sorrow had nearly driven reason from her seat, and melancholy verged upon madness.

I have forced myself to dwell upon these scenes of horror, with whatever pain to my own feelings, because in this favoured country, which the mercy of Heaven has hitherto preserved from being the theatre of war, and from experiencing the calamities which have visited other nations, I have sometimes thought that the blessings of that exemption are but imperfectly felt, and that the sufferings and the dangers of those whose valour and whose blood have been its security and glory, are but faintly understood, and coldly commiserated. I wished that those who had suffered in the cause of their country should be repaid by her gratitude, and that she should learn more justly to estimate " the price of victory." But it is impossible for me to describe, or for imagination to conceive, the horrors of Waterloo!

How gladly would I dwell upon the individual merits of those who fell upon this glorious field, had I but the power to snatch from oblivion one of the many names which ought to be enrolled in the proud list of their country's heroes! In the heat of such a battle, probably thousands have fallen, whose untold deeds surpass all that from childhood our hearts have worshipped.   But that heroic valour and devoted patriotism, which in other days were confined to individuals and signalised their conduct—at Waterloo pervaded every breast. Every private soldier acted like a hero, and thus individual merit was lost in the general excellence, as the beams of the stars are undistinguished in the universal blaze of day.

But it is not only the unrivalled glory of my countrymen in arms, of which I am proud, it is the noble use which they have made of their triumph.   It is not only their irresistible valour in battle, but their unexampled mercy and moderation in victory which exalts them above all other nations.   It has been justly said by those whom they conquered, that no other army than the British could have won the battles of Quatre Bras and Waterloo: and no other army but the British, after such a battle and such a victory, after a long course of incessant warfare, after recent insults and wanton cruelties, and after ages of inveterate hostility and national animosity,—no other army but the British, in such circumstances, would have marched through the heart of that enemy's country, and entered that enemy's capital, as the British army marched through France and entered Paris.

We have only to remember what has invariably been the conduct of the French armies in their march through the countries they have conquered.   We have only to picture to ourselves what *would* have been their conduct, if they had triumphantly marched through England, and we shall then be able to appreciate the meritorious moderation of the British army.   No plundered towns, no burning villages, no ruined houses marked their course ; no outrage, no cruelty nor violence disgraced their triumphant progress. The French people received from their enemies that mercy which was denied them by their own soldiers. There is not a spot on the earth, from the burning sands of Egypt to the frozen deserts of Russia—from the Black Sea to the Pillars of Hercules—from the coasts of the Baltic to the shores of the Mediterranean, where the name of Frenchman and of Napoleon Buonaparte is not dreaded and detested. Wherever the power of Buonaparte has been known, or his dominion felt, his name is uttered with execrations. Wherever he has gone, his path, like that of the pestiferous serpent, has been traced by misery and desolation. But it is a proud reflection to every British heart, that there is not a country of the civilised world where England is not mentioned with respect and gratitude, and the very name of Englishman coupled with blessings.

I am too sensible of my own incompetency, and too conscious of my want of knowledge, to attempt to give any account of the battle itself. The deeds of my countrymen I can only admire—I am not qualified to record them. Abler pens than mine must do justice to the events of this day of glory, which I cannot recal to memory without tears: but it was impossible to stand on the field where thousands of my gallant countrymen had fought and conquered, and bled and died—and where their heroic valour had won for England her latest, proudest wreath of glory—without mingled feelings of triumph, pity, enthusiasm, and admiration, which language is utterly unable to express.

I stood alone upon the spot so lately bathed in human blood—where more than two hundred thousand human beings had mingled together in mortal strife: I cast my eyes upon the ruined hovels immortalised by the glorious achievements of my gallant countrymen. I recalled to mind their invincible constancy—their undaunted intrepidity—their heroic self-devotion in the hour of trial—their magnanimity and mercy in the moment of victory: I cast my eyes upon the tremendous graves at my feet, filled with the mortal remains of heroes.—Silence and desolation now reigned on this wide field of carnage: the scattered relics of recent slaughter and devastation covered the sun-burnt ground; the gales of heaven, as they passed me, were tainted with the effluvia of death. I shuddered at the thought that, beneath the clay on which I stood, the best and bravest of human hearts reposed in death. Oh! surely in such a moment and on such a spot, " some human tears might fall and be forgiven!"

Alas! those for whom I mourned sleep in death—and in vain for them are the tears, the praise, or the gratitude of their country: but though their bodies may moulder in the tomb, and their ashes, mingled with the dust, be scattered unnoticed by the winds of winter, their names and their deeds shall never perish—they shall live for ever in the remembrance of their country, and the tears which pity—gratitude—admiration—wring from every British heart, shall hallow their bloody and honourable grave. On earth they shall receive the noblest meed of praise; and oh! may we not, without impiety or presumption, indulge the hope, that in heaven the crown of glory and immortality awaits those who fell in the field of honour, and who in the discharge of their last and noblest duty to their country, " resigned their spirit unto Him that gave it?"

It was with difficulty I could tear myself from the spot—but after casting one long and lingering look upon the wood-crowned hill of Hougoumont, the shattered walls of La Haye Sainte, the hamlet of La Belle Alliance, the woods of Frischermont, the broken hedge in front of which Sir Thomas Picton's division had been stationed, and which was doubly interesting from the remembrance that it was there that gallant and lamented general had fought and fallen ; and after giving one last glance at the ever memorable tree beneath which I stood, I joined my brother and sister, who had been taking sketches at a little distance, and set off with them to Mont St. Jean—lightened of the load of my cuirass, which a little girl, who before the battle had been one of the inhabitants of La Haye Sainte, joyfully carried to the village for half a franc.

On our return we entered the farm-house where Major L. had been conveyed when wounded. The farm-house and offices enclose a court into which the windows of the house look. It is only one story high, and consists of three rooms, one through another. Not only these rooms, but the barns, out-houses, and byres were filled with wounded British officers, many of whom died here before morning.

In that last tremendous attack which took place towards the close of the day, before the arrival of the Prussians (but which, thanks to British valour, was wholly unsuccessful), the battle extended even here. The French suddenly turned the fire of nearly the whole of their artillery against this part of our position, in front of Mont St. Jean, and a general charge of their infantry and cavalry advanced, under cover of this tremendous cannonade, to the attack, Weakened as our army had been in this quarter with the immense loss it had sustained, they expected it to give way instantly, and that they should be able to force their way to Brussels. The Belgians fled at this tremendous onset. The British stood firm and undaunted, contesting every inch of ground. Every little rise was taken and retaken. The

French and English, intermingled with each other, fought man to man, and sword to sword, around these walls, and in this court, while cannon-shot thundered against the walls of the house, and shells broke in at the windows of the rooms crowded with wounded. Such of the officers as it was possible to remove were carried out beneath a shower of musketry. But our troops maintained their ground in spite of the immense numbers of the enemy, and of a most tremendous and incessant fire ; and after a long and desperate contest, the French were completely repulsed and driven back. They never for a moment gained possession even of this farm-house, much less of the village of Mont St. Jean, to which indeed the battle never extended. Some cannon-balls indeed were lodged in the walls of the cottages, but the action took place entirely in front of the village, and its possession was never therefore disputed.

The farmer's wife had actually remained in this farm-house during the whole of this tremendous battle, quite alone, shut up in her own room, or rather garret. There she sat the whole day, listening to the roar of the cannon, in solitude and silence, unable to see anything, or to hear any account of what was passing. It seemed to me that the utmost ingenuity of man could not have devised a more terrible punishment than this woman voluntarily inflicted upon herself. When I asked her what could have been her motives for remaining in such a dreadful situation, she said that she stayed to take care of her property—that all she had in the world consisted in cows and calves, in poultry and pigs—and she thought if she went away and left them, she should lose them all—and perhaps have her house and furniture burnt. She seemed to applaud herself not a little for her foresight. If the French, however, had been victorious instead of the English, the woman, as well as her hens and chickens, would have been in rather an awkward predicament.

Her husband first told me this story, which I could scarcely credit till she herself confirmed it. But he, honest man ! had wisely run away before the battle had begun, leaving his wife, his pigs, and poultry to take care of themselves. She said she stayed in her room all that night, and never came down till the following morning, when all the surviving wounded officers had been removed, but the bodies of those who had expired during the night still remained, and the floors of all the rooms were stained with blood. She seemed very callous to their fate, and to the sufferings of the wounded; and very indifferent about everything except her hens and chickens. She led me to a little miserable dark cow-house, where General Cooke(or Cock, as she called him) had remained a considerable time when wounded, and it seemed to be a sort of gratification to her, that a British general had been in her cow-house.

Leaving this farm-house, we walked through the village of Mont St. Jean, and stopped at the little inn, where we found the rest of the party busily employed upon every kind of eatable the house afforded, which consisted of brown bread, and butter and cheese—small beer, and still smaller wine. Although I had rejected with abhorrence at Château Hougoumont a proposal of eating, which some one had ventured unadvisedly to make; and though it did seem to me upon the field of battle that I should never think of eating again, yet no sooner did I cast my eyes upon these viands than I pounced upon them, as a falcon does upon its prey, and devoured them with nearly as much voracity. They seemed to me to be delicious; and the brown bread and butter, especially, were incomparable.

M

The woman of the house and her two daughters, who were industriously employed in plain needlework, related to us with great naïveté all the terrors they had suffered, and all the horrors they had seen. Like all the other inhabitants of the village, they had fled the day before the battle—not into the woods, but to a place, the name of which I do not remember, but which they said was very far off ("bien loin").

Several cannon-balls had lodged in the walls about this house, although it was at the extremity of the village, farthest from the field. Having finished our frugal repast, for which these kind and simple people asked a most trifling recompense, we left Mont St. Jean, passed through the village of Waterloo for the last time, and returned to Brussels with an impression on our minds, from our visit to the field of Waterloo, which no time can efface.

It was on Wednesday, the 19th of July, that we learnt the astonishing news that Napoleon Buonaparte had surrendered himself to the British, and was actually a prisoner on board the Bellerophon. An aide-de-camp of the King of France, going express to the King of Holland at the Hague, was the bearer of this important intelligence. It was communicated to us by General Murray, who came in with a countenance radiant with joy, and scarcely could my sister and I, in our transports, refrain from embracing the good old general. He had himself seen the aide-de-camp of Louis XVIII.; yet this news was so unexpected, so wonderful—and above all so good; that scarcely could it be credited. Could it indeed be possible that Napoleon—the dreaded Napoleon—was really a prisoner to the English! All ranks of people were breathless with expectation, and with trembling eagerness and anxious inquiries awaited further intelligence. In a few hours it was confirmed beyond

a possibility of doubt.—" Buonaparte est pris!—il est pris!
—c'est vrai—c'est bien vrai!" cried M. Weerid, the Belgic
gentleman in whose house Major L. was an inmate, bursting
into his room with a turbulence of joy ill-suited to the
suffering state of our poor wounded friend. The loud acclamations of the populace—the ejaculations of thanksgiving
and tears of joy which burst from the women—and the curses
which were freely bestowed on him by the men—proved the
strength of their terror, and the bitterness of their detestation.

It was our fate to be the bearers of this intelligence almost
the whole way through Belgium. So slowly does news
travel in this country, that although it had arrived in Brussels at five o'clock in the afternoon, and we did not set off
till eight the following morning, no rumours of it had been
received in any of the towns or villages through which we
passed; and we even found the good people of Ghent in
profound ignorance of it. But the Belgians were slow of
belief, and the transport and the vociferous joy with which
it was uniformly received at first, were generally followed
by doubts and fears, and fervent wishes for its truth.

At the inn at Alost we found a party comfortably sitting
down to dinner at twelve o'clock, at the well-spread Table
d'Hôte. No sooner had I mentioned this news than knives
and forks were thrown down, plates and dishes abandoned.
An old fat Belgic gentleman, overturning his soup plate,
literally jumped for joy; another, more nimble, began to
caper up and down the room. A corpulent lady, in attempting to articulate her transport, was nearly choked, like little
Hunchback, with a fish-bone; and the demonstrations of joy
shown by the rest of the party were not less extravagant.
One old man, however, shook his head in sign of incredulity, and said with fervour, when I assured him that Buona-

parte was really a prisoner to the English, "that he should have lived long enough if he ever lived to see that day." Nothing amused me more, however, than the squall set up by an old country-woman, who shook my hand till she nearly wrung it off, and then, shocked at what she had done, burst forth into apologies to me, exclamations of joy, and abuse of Buonaparte, all in a breath.

To my cost, however, the official account of this important news did arrive at Ghent, just after I had gone to bed. It had been more than twenty-four hours on its way, travelling at the rate of about a mile an hour; and much did I wish that it had been longer, for neither peace nor repose was now to be had. Bonfires were lighted, guns fired, squibs and crackers let off in the streets, rockets sent up to the clouds, and both heaven and earth disturbed by the uproar. Not satisfied with this, they took it into their heads to keep up a firing with muskets under my windows; and the inhabitants and the English soldiers, royally drunk and loyally noisy, vied with each other in singing or rather roaring out the most discordant strains ; and "God save the King," in English, and a variety of Belgic songs in low Dutch, were sung all at once, with the most patriotic perseverance, in the streets. By the time these outrageously loyal people found their way to bed, it was nearly time for me to get up, which I did at five o'clock, in order to see a very fine cabinet of paintings. The old Flemish gentleman to whom they belonged, not satisfied with giving me permission to see them, had the politeness to rise at that unseasonable hour, in order that he might be ready to receive me, and to show them to me himself. What English gentleman would have got out of his bed before six o'clock in order to show his collection of paintings to a foreigner, a person of no distinction, of whom he knew nothing, who had no introduction to him, whom he had never seen before, and would most probably never see again?

Next day at nine o'clock we embarked from Ostend for England in a large packet crowded with passengers. We set sail with a favouring gale, but the winds and the waves maintained their usual capricious and inconstant character, and after a succession of calms, contrary winds, and opposing tides, we found ourselves, late on the evening of the second day, at anchor within sight of the harbour of Margate, but without a hope of reaching it till the following morning. In order to escape spending another night on board, we embraced the expedient of committing ourselves to a little boat, in which it seemed invariably to be our fate to end all our voyages.

We were rowed ashore, and landed in the dark, at past eleven o'clock at night, upon the slippery and weed-covered rocks of Margate, exactly six weeks after we had landed in the same manner, at the same hour, and the same day of the week, on the deep and deserted sands of Ostend. In that six weeks what a change had taken place! When I left England, Buonaparte was the terror of the world—Europe was arming against him, and his threatening hosts were ready to overwhelm it again with ruin. When I returned, these tremendous armies were defeated and scattered—the victorious troops of England were in the capital of France; and Buonaparte himself, fallen from the highest imperial throne of the universe to the lowest abyss of fortune, was a prisoner on board a British ship of war, and a suppliant to the mercy of my country!

Events so extraordinary and improbable, and changes so sudden and so wonderful, seemed to outrun the rapidity of imagination itself, and to exceed the limits of possibility.

The past seemed like a dream. Scarcely, on retrospection, could we believe it to be real, or be convinced that the scenes we had witnessed, since our departure from England, had not been the illusions of fancy, or the " baseless fabric of a vision." They bore more resemblance to the shifting and imaginary scenes represented on the stage, than to events which had actually happened on the great theatre of the world. It had indeed been a great and a bloody tragedy, and it had been our lot to witness it from the first to the last scene. It began at our entrance, it finished at our departure from Brussels. The news of Buonaparte having attacked the Prussians reached Brussels at the very moment of our arrival—the news of his surrender to the British was received the night before we left it.

In that six weeks the work of an age had been accomplished; an usurper had been dethroned; a monarch had been restored; a kingdom had been lost and won; a war had begun and ended; peace had revisited the world; and justice —strict, impartial justice—had descended upon the head of the guilty. And all this was the work of England !

Yet it has been asked—and I have often heard the question slightingly repeated by my own countrymen—" And what, after all, has England gained for years of war and bloodshed but glory?" I might answer that she has gained security, peace, and prosperity for the world, and for herself, besides, the highest place among nations: but granting that she had only gained glory—what, I ask in return, could she gain that is equivalent to it? What is there on earth to be compared to it?

> " Is aught on earth so precious and so dear
> As Fame or Honour ? or is aught so bright
> And beautiful as Glory's beams appear,
> Whose goodly light than Phœbus' lamp doth shine more clear ?"
> *Faerie Queen.*

Glory is the highest, the most lasting good. Without it, extent of empire, political greatness, and national prosperity, are but a name; without it, they can have no security, and can command no respect; without it all other possessions are worthless and despicable—unstable and transitory. Fortune may change; arts may perish; commerce may decay; and wealth and power, and dominion and greatness may pass away—but glory is immortal and indestructible, and will last when empires and dynasties are no more.

What gives nations honour and renown in future times but the glory they have acquired? What exalted Greece and Rome to their proud pre-eminence among the nations, and transmitted the lustre of their name to the remotest time? Why does the traveller still traverse distant countries, to explore with hallowed respect their mouldering temples, and linger with silent awe amidst the ruins of the Parthenon, or on the site of the Capitol? Why does generation after generation contemplate with veneration the plains of Marathon, and the heights of Leuctra? Why do they still retrace with enthusiasm the deeds of their departed heroes, and the long catalogue of their ancient glories?—It is to these ancient glories that they owe their present interest and importance. The nations of the East were possessed of unbounded wealth, magnificence, and power—and were long the seats of commerce, of the arts of life, and of learning, when the western world was immersed in ignorance and barbarism.—Yet their antiquities are unexplored — their history neglected—their very existence almost forgotten ; for they have left no proud remembrance, no ray of glory, to immortalise their name.

If it had been extent of empire, or superiority of wealth, that gave nations lasting greatness, Persia would have enjoyed that veneration which is now paid to Athens. If it had been conferred by antiquity, or by being the birth-place of the arts and sciences, Egypt would have stood upon that pedestal of fame which Rome now fills.

Yes! England has nobly fought, triumphantly conquered and well has she been rewarded! She has gained that unalienable, imperishable prize, which neither time nor fortune, nor fate—nor any earthly power can ever wrest from her. She has won the immortal meed! Generations yet unborn shall pride themselves on being the descendants of those who fought and conquered in the righteous cause of Justice, Honour, and Independence, on the plains of Spain, and on the glorious field of Waterloo; and feel the throb of generous enthusiasm and of virtuous patriotism, when they retrace the bright history of their country's achievements.

With these sentiments deeply impressed upon my mind ; with the proud consciousness, that highly as the fame of England had stood in all ages, she had now attained an unparalleled height of greatness and glory; that the ancient triumphs of Cressy, Poictiers, and Agincourt, in one age, of Ramillies, Malplaquet, and Blenheim, in another, had been surpassed in those of Salamanca, Vittoria, and Waterloo, in our own; that her name would descend to the latest times as unrivalled in arms, invincible by land and by sea, and pre-eminent, not only in valour, but in faith and honour—in justice, mercy, and magnanimity, and in public virtue— I returned to my country after all the varying and eventful scenes through which it had been my lot to pass, more proud than when I left it of the name of

AN ENGLISHWOMAN.

A TRIBUTE

TO THE

MEMORY OF THE DUKE OF WELLINGTON.

WRITTEN THE DAY AFTER HIS FUNERAL.

19th November, 1852.

THE great Arthur, Duke of Wellington, whose latest achievements in war form the subject of the preceding pages, is no more. Long, long will the nation mourn the greatest, the most irreparable loss it ever sustained. The last sad and solemn scene has passed away. That great and wondrous man, who was its stay, its pride and glory, has been borne to his honoured tomb, amidst those splendid obsequies and funeral pomps with which his grateful country vainly sought to evince her unbounded admiration, her devoted love, and her profound veneration, for him who was her deliverer and preserver; to whom she owed her unprecedented triumphs in war—her prolonged blessings in peace.

" His funeral pall has been borne by nations—not by the nations he enslaved, but the nations he liberated;—the truncheons of eight armies have dropped from his grasp, and they were borne in the funeral procession by the companions and allies of his arms and victories."* But, nobler far, he was followed to the grave by the blessings and the tears of millions; and he, alone, amidst all the great generals and conquerors of the earth, merits the proud eulogium, that he was at once a true patriot and a benefactor to his species.

Eloquence has vainly exhausted itself in enumerating his merits and services; but words are powerless to speak his

* *Times,* November 18th, 1852.

praises. They are felt in the hearts of the people of England. Never did a chieftain, a conqueror, a hero, descend to the tomb so universally honoured and lamented. All ranks, all ages, all parties, unite in one unanimous sense of sorrow and bereavement. Every man seems to feel that he, personally, has lost a benefactor, a protector—almost a parent. And as the light of the sun is not missed until it is withdrawn, so even his value was not perhaps fully felt until he was lost.

But he is gone! "Quenched is that light which was the leading star to guide every Briton on the path of duty and honour."* His name is surrounded by a pure halo of glory—not that ordinary vulgar glory which is the meed of the mere conqueror. No! the "hero of a hundred fights," who never knew defeat, sought not, valued not such glory; nay, more, he despised it; he never even named "its very name."† His watchword was Duty, and the path of duty, honour, and patriotism, he trod. What a striking contrast did his career present to that of Napoleon, who sought that vain, false glory, through fields of fire and carnage, crushing the nations beneath his iron yoke, to aggrandise his selfish ambition, and reign the despot of a devastated world! How striking is the fact, that at the very time when, by the mysterious decree of Providence, a Buonaparte was sent to desolate and enslave the world, a Wellesley was given to save and deliver it!—the one, the Destroyer; the other, the Preserver. They seemed like the Incarnate Principles of Evil and of Good; but the Good

---

* Lord Lovaine's speech, November 12th.
† It is well known that the word "Glory" does not once occur in the multifarious dispatches of the Duke of Wellington.

triumphed: the conqueror and deliverer of distracted and bleeding Europe became its Pacificator; and through long years of peace and prosperity the nations which he saved from tyranny and ruin, have had reason to bless the name of Wellington.

Will it yet be permitted to one British heart—simply " An Englishwoman," who witnessed the most eventful scenes of his glorious campaigns, and proudly watched from first to last his high unblemished career—to offer, with the deepest veneration, a humble tribute of high and holy admiration upon the tomb of that hero whom, through life, her heart has worshipped.

The ONE TRUE HERO! unequalled in the annals of history—unsurpassed even in the creations of Romance; He, who never headed the battalions of his countrymen except in a just and righteous cause, and never once failed to lead them on to victory and honour; He, who was not only the " Victor of Victors," the greatest of Conquerors, but also the greatest Pacificator the world ever saw—for he used the triumphs of War only to obtain the blessings of Peace;—He, whose first thought in victory was mercy, whose first care was to ensure, not the spoils, but the protection of the vanquished;—He, who, when he sheathed his conquering sword, consecrated the powers of his mighty genius, his mind, and life, to the welfare of his country; who worked her weal through evil report and good report, unmoved by the cabals of Faction, the intrigues of Power, and the slanders of Malignity;—He, whose Spirit, whilst he lived, was our Shield and Buckler, our Stay and Support; his counsels our best resource; his name our tower of strength; and his very existence our surest defence.

Alas, for England! Woe! woe to our country! The grave has closed over him; but his sacred ashes shall still guard our land. Around his honoured tomb every British heart will rally to rout and vanquish the hostile foe who dares to set foot on British ground. Every heart will be roused, every arm raised to repel the insult. His name shall be our everlasting panoply of defence; his life, his example, his memory, shall live in our hearts, and to the latest posterity England's proudest boast shall be the name of Wellington.

APPENDIX.

A. (p. 44).

The desertion of General Bourmont did not take place during the Battle of Quatre Bras, but on the day before. He and his Staff joined the Prussian General Ziethen as the French were advancing on Charleroi, on June 15. The mistake, however, is hardly the writer's fault, as Sir F. Head, the English authority for the statement, misprints the date. (See Hooper's *Waterloo*, p. 68.)

B. (p. 93).

The decisive part which the Prussian army played in the Battle of Waterloo is often overlooked, as it is here. Readers must bear in mind that the junction of the two armies of the Allies was preconcerted by Wellington and Blücher, and that the battle would not have been fought under other circumstances. It is true that the Prussian advance from Wavre, whence it had retreated after the Battle of Ligny on the 16th, was delayed, whereby an undue strain was placed upon and nobly borne by the English infantry, but the first Prussian corps under Bülow was known to be approaching by three o'clock. Their advance on the village of Planchenoit, on the right of the French position, caused Napoleon to detach to his right 16,000 French troops, out of the 72,000 with which he began the battle, and at last engaged his attention so far as that he left Ney to conduct the attack upon Wellington's army. Though it may be true, as

Mrs. Eaton states, that the Prussians did not "make their appearance" (*i.e.* to the British troops) till seven o'clock (p. 130), they were nevertheless in conflict with the French for some hours before, and considerably modified their attack on Wellington's position.

C. (p. 145).

The allegations of cowardice brought against Napoleon at the time, and frequently repeated, do not meet with the slightest support from accurate historians. It is almost certain that when Wellington, on the 17th, withdrew his army from Quatre Bras to the position in which he accepted battle on the following day, Napoleon was with the head of the French column which followed up the retreat, and was within cannon shot of the British artillery and of Lord Uxbridge, who commanded the cavalry.

At the close of the Battle of Waterloo he showed no lack of courage. "During the attack of the Imperial Guard he had ridden as far as the orchard of La Haye Sainte; when the Guard recoiled he had rallied them; when the 52nd and other regiments of the brigade pursued so promptly he had gradually fallen back with the steadier masses of the fugitives, surrounded by the truly *dévourés* of those days, the veterans of the Guard."—*Hooper*, p. 238.

It was only when the Prussians, almost fresh upon the field, undertook the pursuit, that he diverged from the press and rapidly made his way to Charleroi, where he obtained a carriage.

D. (p. 148).

The celebrated order of Wellington to the Guards is perhaps, in its popular form, not quite authentic. When towards the close of the battle Ney, unhorsed, was leading the column of the Old Guard up the slope of the British position, behind the crest of which the British infantry was lying, Wellington said, " Up, Guards, and make ready ! " they " sprang to their feet within fifty yards of the astonished French, and poured in a volley which struck the column like a bolt of iron . . . and when the Duke cried, ' Charge ! ' and the British Guards dashed forward with a cheer, Ney's veterans broke and fled."—*Hooper*, p. 231. The approach of cavalry caused the British to retreat to their position on the hill, but in the meantime the second column of the French Guard had been routed by a bold and skilful charge of the 52nd Regiment, followed up by cavalry, whilst the Prussians were successfully pushing back the right wing of the French. Then the English leader saw that his time, at last, was come. To quote again Mr. Hooper's stirring description : " On the ridge near the Guards, his figure standing out amidst the smoke against the bright north-western sky, Wellington was seen to raise his hat with a noble gesture, the signal for the wasted line of heroes to sweep like a dark wave from their coveted position, and roll out their lines and columns over the plain. With a pealing cheer, the whole line advanced just as the sun was sinking, and the Duke, sternly glad, but self-possessed, rode off into the thick of the fight, attended by only one officer, almost the last of the splendid squadron which careered around him in the morning."—P. 234.

E. (p. 149).

Though the meeting of Wellington and Blücher at La Belle Alliance has been made the subject of a well-known picture, it is not founded on fact. The actual meeting took place nearer Rossomme, some distance further south on the Charleroi road, along which the routed army was struggling. From this point the pursuit was left to Blücher's troops.

LONDON :

PRINTED BY WILLIAM CLOWES AND SONS, LIMITED,

STAMFORD STREET AND CHARING CROSS.

www.ingramcontent.com/pod-product-compliance
Lightning Source LLC
Chambersburg PA
CBHW020536270326
41927CB00006B/600